MONEY:

The Right Way to Think about it & the Right Way to Use it

MONEY:

THE RIGHT WAY TO THINK ABOUT IT & THE RIGHT WAY TO USE IT

Christopher W.C. Salley

XULON PRESS

Xulon Press
2301 Lucien Way #415
Maitland, FL 32751
407.339.4217
www.xulonpress.com

Cover Design and Chapter Illustrations by Kamaca Champion

Unless otherwise indicated, Scripture quotations taken from the Holy Bible, New International Version (NIV). Copyright © 1973, 1978, 1984, 2011 by Biblica, Inc.™. Used by permission. All rights reserved.

Scripture quotations taken from the King James Version (KJV)–*public domain.*

Printed in the United States of America.

ISBN-13: 978-1-6322-1992-3
Ebook: 978-1-6322-1993-0

<u>Book Dedication</u>

To my parents who give me great encouragement
To my wife who gives me great joy
To my children who give me great hope

TABLE OF CONTENTS

Introduction. ix

Chapter 1: Show Me the Money. 1

Chapter 2: You'd Better Recognize 19

Chapter 3: I'm Just Waiting to Exhale 41

Chapter 4: Giving for a Living .71

Chapter 5: The Greatness of Giving 89

Chapter 6: The Biblical Wisdom
　　　　　of Saving and Investing 113

Chapter 7: Do the Right Thing 153

Chapter 8: How Then Should We Live?. 173

INTRODUCTION

T o honor God with our resources. Every believer should have that desire in gratitude to the many blessings that God has bestowed. He has given us time, talent, and treasure, and He expects us to use them wisely.

However, when it comes particularly to our money, we often fall well short of reaching this goal. Our consumer-driven culture has made most of us prone to the greed, immediate gratification, and lack of contentment of the American lifestyle. Many Americans, including Christians, struggle with high levels of credit card debt, unwieldy home mortgages and multiple car payments. Hard times also come with unexpected medical bills or obligations to care for extended family members with little or no savings set aside.

Our problem is primarily spiritual. Fortunately, the prescription is the biblical truth of stewardship. Believers can find answers to every challenge in the wisdom of the Scriptures. God's Word is a guidebook, not a rule book. In the Word of God, you and I find sufficiently detailed insight to live abundant and fruitful lives.

This book is for believers who want sound, biblical guidance in the area of finances. The book seeks to be practical without being technical. As a finance professional in the marketplace for over thirty years as well as a leader in pastoral ministry for over twenty-five years, I can offer a key vantage point: a strong emphasis on the exposition of biblical texts while applying the Word to our everyday lives. I provide a money recipe as well as targeted recommendations for changing behavioral patterns so we can honor God fully with our resources. Given the challenges Christians face in our economy and our culture, *Money* should be both timely and refreshing as is its distinct call: You can find contentment through eliminating debt, increasing your giving and savings, and reducing your consumption.

To help achieve these goals, you will learn in the following chapters the money recipe that will strengthen your financial livelihood and allow you to honor God with your resources. Here is a summary of the chapters.

Chapter 1 introduces the concept of stewardship by exploring the parable of the ten talents in Luke 19:10-24. A close examination of the relationship between the servants and the master in this text helps to emphasize the critical truth that we are managers and not owners of the resources we have. Chapter 2 presents some basic principles of stewardship through the exposition of a second parable, that of the shrewd manager in Luke 16:1–14. Stewardship is a truth that must be embraced for it will change one's outlook, plans and situation. Active application of these stewardship principles will result in true wisdom, true riches and true service.

Beginning with chapter 3, we explore a new money allocation recipe, with debt as the first parameter. Debt is a spiritual issue that is linked to greed and goes directly to the heart of contentment. Several signs of a person with a debt problem are discussed, as well as several steps to take to climb out of indebtedness. This recipe becomes the focus for correctly honoring God with one's resources.

Chapters 4 and 5 focus on giving as the second parameter in the money recipe through an exposition of II Corinthians 8:1-15. The mindset of giving includes an understanding that giving is about sacrifice, selflessness, sharing and submission. We learn the mystery of giving—that giving is truly about grace, not about money. Chapter 5 emphasizes the wisdom of the tithe as the appropriate guide and expression for honoring the Lord with our giving.

Chapter 6 focuses on the third parameter of the money recipe, which is saving and investing. We explore the subject through an examination of threes: three principles, three practices, three priorities, three problems and three pursuits.

Chapter 7, "Do the Right Thing," details the believer's responsibilities before God, as it relates to government, through an exposition of Romans 13:1-14. Support of the government through taxes and revenues is the fourth parameter in the money recipe.

Chapter 8 discusses the last parameter in the money recipe, consumption, and leaves the reader with five points of emphasis in terms of moving forward as stewards.

To be good stewards, you and I must know the right way to think about our money, as well as know the right way to use it. Join me as we learn how we can use our resources to advance God's kingdom and bring glory to Him.

Fall 2020 Update

This book was originally finished in 2011, although for a number of reasons it has not been released until now. After retiring in 2007 to full-time ministry, I returned to the financial marketplace taking a job in private equity in 2012. I write in Chapter 6 about God leading to me leave my job for full-time ministry. I also write now that I believe He led me to return to the marketplace. Things did not go according to <u>my</u> plans, but I am confident that I am still in the center of God's will for my life and I am still honoring Him by practicing faithful stewardship. My life journey has been quite interesting, and I look forward to the chapters God writes next for me!

CHAPTER I:
SHOW ME THE MONEY

how me the money. A line made famous by Rod Tidwell in "Jerry McGuire." The sum total of his experience was you've got to be about the business of showing me the money. In the body of Christ, there are so many of us as we approach this subject of stewardship, who are under the impression that "show me the money" is what we are supposed to be saying to God. Now, hopefully none of those folks are reading this book. Not us. But I would dare to tell you that many times that is how we act and that is how we posture ourselves. We say to God, "Show me the money." We do not even realize that God is really saying to you, and to me, "You show *me* the money."

It's interesting that anytime we start talking about this subject of stewardship, particularly money, we get uncomfortable. Why do we uncomfortable when we start talking about the money? Because God can see what you <u>value</u> by what you <u>prioritize</u>. He has set it up in such a way that treasure, time, and talent are the things that He is looking for us to effectively manage and most of us have not gotten it right.

The parable of the ten pounds has direct application for us today in the area of stewardship, so let's look at it in Luke 19:

> **11 While they were listening to this, he went on to tell them a parable, because he was near Jerusalem and the people thought that the kingdom of God was going to appear at once. 12 He said: "A man of noble birth**

went to a distant country to have himself appointed king and then to return. [13] So he called ten of his servants and gave them ten minas. `Put this money to work,' he said, `until I come back.'

This nobleman *(who is a figure of Jesus Christ)* went to receive a kingdom and return. The Greek word used for servants is *doulos*, which is better rendered slaves or those that had dedicated their lives to the nobleman. He gave them each some money and told them to occupy until he returned. A pound was worth about 3 months wages. Now, how many people would like, no matter what you make, to get in one chunk three months of your annual income? Wouldn't that be nice? Unfortunately, the way many of us operate, a circumstance like that would end in disaster. We would consider it a windfall and spend it on frivolous items that we did not need. Saving or responsible investing would never enter our minds.

Think it of this way, if you were a second-grade schoolteacher, you could say to your class, "Here's some paper, here's some glue, here's some scissors and here's some crayons. I have to go down to the principal's office for a few minutes, so occupy (or use your imaginations to make a picture of something you would like to share with the class using the items on your desk) until I come back." Now what would be your expectation? What are you saying when you say occupy, until I come back? You're saying that I have given you construction paper, I have given you glue, I have given you crayons, I have given you scissors (Oh Lord!), what I don't expect when I come back is to see that a little boy has cut off the hair of a little girl with the scissors provided. What I don't expect is globs of glue all over people's faces, construction paper balled up and cast all around the room and broken crayons being used as projectiles *(I can hear all the school teachers saying that's exactly what you should have expected since you left those kids alone without supervision! Work with me).* That is not what you mean when you say occupy. You expect that when you come back you will see something created, something beautiful, something more than what you left them with. You are expecting to see some pictures, or some drawings, you're expecting to see children sitting orderly in their seats. And if you did not think they could handle the responsibility, you wouldn't have left them.

When the nobleman left his servants, he gave them something that had ***desirability***. It had value. He gave them three months worth of wages. He also left them something that had some ***capability***. It was useful. In addition, he left them instructions when he said to them occupy until I come. Verse 14 continues the story:

> **"But his subjects hated him and sent a delegation after him to say, `We don't want this man to be our king.'**

Now we see that there are some new characters in the story. There are enemies who hate the master. The presence of enemies should not be a shock to anybody who understands the spiritual warfare the believer has to wage (cf. John 15:19-20, I Peter 5:8). You know enemies are coming, you know they are out there, and as soon as the master leaves, they want to let the servants know that they are opposed to the master. Still, the text says that these are the master's citizens, even though they do not realize it. These are under the nobleman's rule because the kingdom for which he is leaving and will receive, is greater than the kingdom that he's in (cf. Philippians 2:9-11). Yet these citizens hated him and declared that he would not reign over them. The Scripture continues:

> [15] **"He was made king, however, and returned home. Then he sent for the servants to whom he had given the money, in order to find out what they had gained with it.** [16] **"The first one came and said, `Sir, your mina has earned ten more.'** [17] **" `Well done, my good servant!' his master replied. `Because you have been trustworthy in a very small matter, take charge of ten cities.'**
>
> [18] **"The second came and said, `Sir, your mina has earned five more.'** [19] **"His master answered, `You take charge of five cities.'**

When Jesus returns, he wants to know what everybody has gained. He gave each and every one of them three months' wages. The servants are not in a position to ask Him to show them the money. The master told them to occupy so he looks at them and says, "Show *me* the money!" In other words, "What did you do with what I gave you?"

The first servant steps up and it seems like he did all right. He told his master that he turned his one pound into ten pounds. The master was indeed pleased and gave him authority over ten cities. So the servant goes from being in control of three months' wages to now, because of his faithfulness, being in charge of ten cities. With this gift, the master is really saying, "You've done your job because you turned one into ten. And if you can turn one into ten, I'm going to be able to trust you with real riches, and with real responsibility."

So when the servant comes back to his master with ten pounds, he was putting in the work. The master knows the enemy is out there. He knows that the servant had to walk through enemy territory to get done what he needed to do. The same is true for the second servant the master saw. He was also pleasing as he turned the one pound into five pounds. He gained increase and he was rewarded in proportion to what he had done.

Not only did the nobleman give his servants something with ***desirability***, and ***capability***, he gave them something that had ***accountability***. Although he gave money to ten, he only makes an example of three. The third servant appears starting in verse 20:

> **20 "Then another servant came and said, `Sir, here is your mina; I have kept it laid away in a piece of cloth. 21 I was afraid of you, because you are a hard man. You take out what you did not put in and reap what you did not sow.' 22 "His master replied, `I will judge you by your own words, you wicked servant! You knew, did you, that I am a hard man, taking out what I did not put in, and reaping what I did not sow? 23 Why then didn't you put my money on deposit, so that when I came back, I could have collected it with interest?' 24 "Then he said to those standing by, `Take his mina away from him and give it to the one who has ten minas.'**

You know what I call the conversation that this servant had with his master? Church talk. See, this guy had not done

6

anything. He received a pound and turns around and gives a pound right back. But he would not just admit that he had done nothing. He did not say, "Master, I didn't negotiate, I didn't cut any deals, I didn't try to invest the money and get a return on it." He figured that kind of honestly would get him nowhere. So he decided, "When I am in the house around the other servants I know how to say the right things so people *think* I know what I'm doing, and people *think* I'm being faithful, that people *think* that I've got it all together. The third servant knew how to get up and say "Bless the Lord, oh, my soul, and all that is within me, bless His holy name." He knew how to get up and say "I'm wrapped up, tied up and tangled up in Jesus, and I'm saved, sanctified and filled with the Holy Ghost, and going on to press my claim in Jesus name!"

Now, there is nothing wrong with these familiar refrains that many of us have heard in church. But church talk separated from church walk is useless. This guy said with his walk, I am not doing anything. I am not taking any risk. I am not leaving the house. But when he comes back, I will just say something that sounds good like I always do. It is clear he didn't lose any money, but he surely did not make any money. He did not *show* the money, he *hid* the money.

And what did the Scripture say happened to him? He was judged a wicked servant based upon the very things he said he did. He hid his time, he hid his talent and he hid his treasure. Effectively he said to his master, "I know you gave me something that had desirability and capability, and I even knew that there was going to be accountability, but I did not do anything." The master told the third servant that he could have at least put what he was given in a money market or interest-bearing checking account. He could have taken some risk or done something. Unfortunately, that would have required the servant to actually leave the house.

See, many of us like to talk the talk, but never ever, ever walk the walk. Never. Many of us are scared to leave the house and many of us think that we can get the job done by sitting up under one another saying, "Bless the Lord, oh, my soul."

Now, do not you get confused in any way and think that there is a works-based faith that I'm trying to advance here. My response to you (like the Apostle Paul would say) is God forbid! That is not what I'm saying at all. He called him a wicked *servant*, not an enemy, which indicates that there is still relationship. What I am reminding you about is in line with James 2:14-18, which says:

> **14 What good is it, my brothers, if a man claims to have faith but has no deeds? Can such faith save him? 15 Suppose a brother or sister is without clothes and daily food. 16 If one of you says to him, "Go, I wish you well; keep warm and well fed," but does nothing about his physical needs, what good is it? 17 In the same way, faith by itself, if it is not accompanied by action, is dead. 18 But someone will say, "You have faith; I have deeds." Show me your faith without deeds, and I will show you my faith by what I do.**

So it's not a choice between faith and works, but a demonstration of faith *by* works.

Ephesians 2:8-10 further speaks to this issue:

8 For it is by grace you have been saved, through faith—and this not from yourselves, it is the gift of God— 9 not by works, so that no one can boast. 10 For we are God's workmanship, created in Christ Jesus *to do good works*, **which God prepared in advance for us to do.** (*emphasis mine*)

So clearly you do not have to do anything *for* salvation, but you surely have to do something *with* salvation. That is the distinction that's being made here and the foundation of the master's plea to occupy until He comes. The expectation is that you will do something with what you have been given. If you don't, what has been given to you can be taken from you and given to someone else (v. 24). It may seem unfair to you that the servant who already has 10 received the one taken from the third servant, but the nobleman knows what he is doing. The servant with ten pounds has proven himself to be faithful and worthy of trust by his master. If you cannot prove faithful with what God has given you, your expectation should be the same as the result for the wicked servant. Basically, if you do not use it, you can lose it.

How many times is a farmer going to work a patch of land that does not give fruit, especially if he has another patch of land that is working and giving a great yield? At some point as a manner of proper management, that farmer will determine that he needs to focus his efforts in the one area because he sees productivity and move away from the other area since it does not yield anything. Now please know that God has a large reservoir of patience and He also desires that you be productive. Remember the parable of the fig tree in Luke 13:6-9? That fig tree was not producing fruit, and then the owner came by and determined that because of the lack of productivity, the fig tree should simply be cut down. However, the caretaker appealed to the owner to give the tree another year. That reflects the heart of our Lord – He wants you to produce and He patiently gives more time and encouragement for you to do so. However, at some point, he is going to come back, and he will judge by asking that you show him the money—the fruit.

You might be thinking, "Are we still talking about steward-ship?" We are definitely still talking about stewardship. If you can get this concept, it will absolutely change your life. This is one of the most revolutionary things that you will hear, and if you and I can put this into practice, it will shift how you view the entirety of your world. Here it is: **you are a steward, and not an owner**. From the beginning, we were stewards. In the beginning God created the heavens and the earth. God created everything. Did you hear what I said? God created everything and owns everything.

Psalms 24:1 says

> **The earth is the LORD's, and everything in it, the world, and all who live in it;**

I do not care what Tony Montana (*Scarface*) said, the world is not his. I do not care what Nino Brown (*New Jack City*) said, the world isn't his either. You'd better understand, God owns this world and everything in it.

The world is His, so much so that Colossians 1:15 –17 tells us this about Jesus:

> **15 He is the image of the invisible God, the firstborn over all creation. 16 For by him all things were created: things in heaven**

and on earth, visible and invisible, whether thrones or powers or rulers or authorities; all things were created by him and for him. 17 He is before all things, and in him all things hold together.

Scripture is testifying that not only has Christ created everything, he sustains everything. If he took his hand off the world, it would spin out of control. "Gravitational pull" is our explanation of the hand of God keeping the earth right where it is. God makes the seasons change and He makes the earth journey around the sun in 365.25 days. God is the one who keeps all of the planets revolving around the sun in such a way that they never collide and they keep their particular orbit. Isaiah 40:22 reminds us with eloquent prose that it is God who sits enthroned above the circle of the earth and its people are like grasshoppers. It is vitally important that you understand that God is the creator and sustainer of all life. He owns and runs it all.

You may say, well, what about us? God indeed has a place for us. He always has. In time past He said to Himself that He would make a special creature, not like the animals. He decided that He would put His image on that creature and draft him to be a junior partner in the world enterprise that He owns. He decided to hire some help and put them in the garden.

Genesis 1:27-28 says:

27 So God created man in his own image, in the image of God he created him;

male and female he created them. 28 God blessed them and said to them, "Be fruitful

> **and increase in number; fill the earth and subdue it. Rule over the fish of the sea and the birds of the air and over every living creature that moves on the ground."**

To paraphrase, God said, Look, I know you just got on the scene, but understand that I own everything. It's mine. I created it and I sustain it. However, I have a 5-part job description that I want you to execute. 1) Be fruitful, 2) multiply, 3) replenish the earth, 4) subdue it and 5) have dominion. Those are our jobs. That is our assignment. He told Adam and Eve they were being hired as managers. That's what a steward is, a manager.

Before moving to full-time ministry, I professionally managed other people's investments for many years. I also managed process and people on behalf of the person who owned the company. If I ever got that twisted, the owner was in a position to let me know that it was his company and that I worked for him. It's that simple. If you are not cutting the checks, you are not the owner. And I've got news for you; even if you own your own business, you still don't own it. It's God's.

We must stay in touch with this revolutionary concept: You and I don't own anything. The house you have, it's not yours. The clothes? Forget about it. That's like a teenager telling their parent that they own their bedroom. The parent would no doubt declare the child legally insane because that bedroom is in the parent's house. As God sees us going about in our daily lives, pretending like we own stuff, I imagine He's looking at all of us and saying, "Let me help my child understand how this really works." You don't own anything. You may act or think as an owner, but you are only a manager.

Most stewards in the Bible were slaves. For example, Eliazar was Abraham's steward and Joseph was a steward in

Potiphar's house. The Apostle Paul proclaimed to be a slave of Christ and a steward of the mysteries of God (I Corinthians 4:1). Scripture also teaches that bishops and elders are called stewards (Titus 1:7) and as members of the body of Christ we are encouraged to be good stewards of the manifold grace of God (I Peter 4:10). A steward is entrusted with something, but he does not own it. And if you don't own it, that means have to give account for it to the one who does. God is the owner with whom you and I need to be concerned.

Now here is the great thing: if you don't own it, your level of responsibility is different. Think of the employee/employer relationship. In exchange for your productivity, the employer has to give you provision. He says, "I'll give you the tools you need, and I'll take care of paying the bills. Why? Because I own it. I'm just trying to make sure you are productive and in exchange for that productivity I will give you provision."

Our steward/owner relationship with God is no different. You should be excited that you're a steward and not an owner. Because ownership has challenges and pressures that you as a steward don't have to worry about. You don't have to worry about from where the increase is coming. That's the owner's job. And if God can get you what you need out of His infinite supply, what are you worried about? Enjoy your relationship with the Owner by working to get the best result in all that you do.

As a faithful steward you must do three things. First, you must understand what you have been given and then use it. You must *understand your provision*. You and I may not know all that we have when God gave us our "pound" but we must understand that what was given has desirability, capability, and accountability. Maybe that's what happened to the wicked servant. Maybe he threw it in a corner or put it on the shelf because he did not realize the value of it.

Maybe there was one time when you were growing up that you received a birthday card from a relative and you didn't really pay attention to it as you should. You didn't realize there was anything in it until your grandma tells you later, "Now don't spend that money all in one place, here!" Now you scramble back to see what you did with that card. and every birthday after that you open Grandma's card, you make sure you shake it out *and* you look inside the envelope! When you know what you've received is valuable, you treat it differently.

But you and I must understand our provision, and then strive to put our provision to good use. When we understand that God has given us time, talent and treasure, it's valuable. And it's useful. So we want to be accountable to Him for it. When you and I understand that, we'll push through. Who wants to be considered a wicked servant? I don't. Who wants to hear, "I don't have anything for you, because you didn't have anything for me. You didn't show me the money, so I have nothing for you." Do you want that to be your testimony? Rest assured it will all come out when the master returns.

God will be able to tell from the results that you understood and followed these concepts or you didn't. You've got the Word of God, you've got the Holy Spirit and you've got the body of Christ. Those are gifts. If you are not fellowshipping with a church, and if you are not active in a ministry, then you are not occupying until He comes back. He's also given you at least one spiritual gift that He's deposited in you with the expectation of a return. If you are not using that gift to be fruitful and fulfilled in ministry, you're missing out.

The second thing you must do is understand that increase is gained by stepping outside. In other words, *understand your prospects*. The master gave ten pounds, right? And, we know for sure that there was an additional nine from the one servant who turned one into ten, and from the second servant an additional four, who turned one into five, there was that's thirteen additional pounds, for sure. From where did those additional pounds come? Outside of the house. The ten servants could have sat in the house under one another, passing those ten pounds around and it would have been what's known as a zero sum game.

You and I must understand that outside is where you gain the increase. If we stay inside the walls of our churches we will only have ten pounds when He comes. Outside, that's evangelism. Outside, you must meet and greet people, you have to tell other people about Jesus Christ. You must take some risks and you have to put yourself out there. You must take chances like inviting somebody from your job to come to church with you. You must talk to your relative for the third time even though you know she has been hostile to you the last two times you mentioned something about Jesus Christ. That's an outside mentality and it takes an outside mentality to gain pounds.

Have you ever heard of a lifeguard who gets dressed for work but doesn't want to get wet? They put on the swimsuit, rub on the sunscreen, get the little cream for their nose, and think that if anyone needs help it will get done from the beach or the pier. We don't mind throwing a buoy or using a pole but we avoid jumping in at all costs. What if somebody is further away than our reach or equipment? Should we say, oh well, I wish I had a longer pole? Do you refuse to jump in because if you jump, you'll have to start all over again and put the sunscreen and cream back on? Somebody is out there. And they are beyond the rescue pole and the reach of the buoy. What do you need to do? *Jump in. Get wet. It's ok.* If we don't get increase from the outside, we'll never see it.

Lastly, as a steward you must *understand your predicament.* And what is your predicament? Your predicament is the Enemy awaits you out there, he hates you and is trying to destroy your life. He wants to sabotage the reputation of the body of Christ. If you don't understand that, you will not be focused and you will not stand. You'll shrink and will never gain additional pounds of the kingdom.

To sum up this chapter: <u>*You and I are stewards*</u>. God created everything. God sustains everything. Therefore, God owns everything. We don't own anything—not our <u>time</u>, our <u>talent</u>, not our <u>treasure</u>. We're servants of the Most High so we don't even own our lives. And the sooner we get on board with God's program, the better off we'll be.

In Jonah 2, Jonah was in the belly of the whale and right before he got out, he said,

> **8 "Those who cling to worthless idols forfeit the grace that could be theirs. 9 But I, with a song of thanksgiving, will sacrifice to you. What I have vowed I will make good. Salvation comes from the LORD."**

Simply put, those who chase after things that are not true are forfeiting the mercy that is theirs. They're not understanding their provision. They're not understanding their prospects. They're not understanding their predicament. They have forsaken their own mercy. They don't understand that they're stewards, and not owners. But like Jonah you should say, "I'm going to pay what I have vowed. I'm going to stand because I'm committed to this master and I know he's going to return.

Salvation is of the Lord." And when Jonah made that statement, the next verse of Scripture says that the fish vomited him out on dry land! Some of us have been waiting on the Lord for things—for direction, for guidance, and maybe what *He's* waiting for, is not for you to ask him some questions but to provide Him with some answers.

Show Him the money.

Discussion Questions:

1. If you were given a large chunk of money, how would you use it? Looking back on your current spending habits, how quickly would that money disappear? Would the use of that money be wise?

2. What was the difference between the first two servants and the third servant in Luke 19? How did the third servant react to his stewardship?

3. This chapter says we are stewards of God's earth, not owners. What exactly does a steward do? How should this mentality affect a Christian's life?

4. How does the enemy distract you from being a good steward?

CHAPTER 2:
YOU'D BETTER RECOGNIZE

We often say, "You'd better recognize," when somebody is missing what we believe is an obvious point. They don't know "the deal" and we're getting ready to let them know, in a way that they might not like, that we *do* know the deal! Once truth is revealed, you have an opportunity to do one of two things. You either gravitate toward it as truth, or you reject it as falsehood. But you have to make a choice.

Now here's a truth we must each recognize: *stewardship is a truth* that you and I must embrace. When we do, it will change our outlook, plans, and situation.

In Deuteronomy 8:17-18, the Lord gives a warning to the children of Israel.

> **17 You may say to yourself, "My power and the strength of my hands have produced this wealth for me." 18 But remember the LORD your God, for it is he who gives you the ability to produce wealth, and so confirms his covenant, which he swore to your forefathers, as it is today.**

The people hadn't even made it to the Promised Land yet but the Lord needed to remind them to trust Him because He knew how they were. He basically told them, "When you get to the land, and you start eating well from all the land produces, don't forget where you've come from and who is responsible for bringing you to where you are. Remember that you didn't do any of it. I provided all of it for you."

You might say," I'm a self-made person," or "I started a business," or "I put myself through school." My power, my might, my hand got me where I am today. My response to you is *you'd better recognize*! Everything you have comes from God. *Everything*. Everything is His, and when it comes particularly to your resources, it's not that you're giving God 10% (if you are honoring Him with a tithe), *He's allowing you to use 90%*. It's all His. He does not need your check; rather He is trying to teach you to prioritize Him first. This is about putting the spiritual before the material (as Jesus said in Matthew 6:33). God can do more *through* you and *for* you by letting you manage 90%, than you ever could by keeping 100%. God's math works differently.

Accept the concept of stewardship and it will change your outlook. That's because biblical stewardship is a *revolutionary* truth. When you start a revolution in a people, you start first with their minds. In the 1960s when black people began an unprecedented press for change, it wasn't guns that they grabbed; it was books. One black leader, Jesse Jackson, began to encourage black people to say, "Black is Beautiful!" That began to affect the minds of the people. The encouragement was that you have to understand and know that you are beautiful and you're black, and that you're somebody (another phrase made popular by Rev. Jackson). See, a revolution starts with trying to affect somebody's mind; so you must grasp stewardship as a revolutionary truth.

Not only is it a revolutionary truth; stewardship is a *relevant* truth. It should change your plans. When you know you are a steward, you will plan differently and interact differently with the world around you. A steward says: "I'm doing this on behalf of my master who owns everything. He lends it to me. He allows me to use it. And I am accountable to him for everything in my life." *Everything* obviously includes more than just money. For example, I am accountable to God for my physical fitness. Why? My health and strength are a trust that He gives me and therefore I must give an account for how I take care of myself.

What about all the political discussions concerning the environment? The environment is essentially a stewardship issue. Human beings are stewards over the earth (Genesis 1:28), so we must give account to God for how we treat the earth. We are not supposed to abuse the earth or the creatures that are on it. Although we clearly have dominion, we still need to take care of our planet. There is also stewardship over our time, our talent and our relationships. When God tells you to show Him the money, it should be clear that you will give account of everything in your life. Why? Because you are a steward.

The truth that you're a steward is not only revolutionary and relevant, it is also *real*. It will change your situation. You will not only *plan* differently, you will *act* differently. Now, you can do with this truth what you want. But know if you don't grasp it and do what God has instructed in terms of stewardship, then you reject His truth. **You'd better recognize**.

Do you know what a quit claim deed is? A quit claim deed is a legal document that transfers property from one party to another. Once you sign it, you're not claiming the property listed anymore. Hence the name, quit claim. When you retire a mortgage the real question is, where's the deed? The deed runs with the property, so, whoever owns the property possesses the deed. Unfortunately, for most of us, it's still the bank! But one fine day there is a deed that will be transferred to you once you pay off that mortgage. It's yours!

22

Well, you and I need to execute a quit claim deed with the Lord where we transfer all of our property over to Him as a tangible reminder that everything is His and nothing is ours. The quit claim deed would say something like, "I hereby transfer to the Lord the ownership of the following possessions: My house, my car, my time, my talent, my bank account, my investments and all of the other material items in my life." You would sign it as a steward and have a space for a witness who will hold you accountable for the recognition of the Lord's ownership. A document such as this would not be enforceable in a court of law, but simply recognized in the kingdom.

Here's a secret: *Whether you actually sign the quit claim deed or not, it's the truth anyway!* However, this helps you to recognize that stewardship is a <u>revolutionary</u>, <u>relevant</u>, and <u>real</u> truth that has application in your life.

So how does a steward respond to his monetary situations? First off, let's look at Luke 16 to read about another steward and how he handled his money.

Let's look at the text in Luke 16:

1 Jesus told his disciples: "There was a rich man whose manager was accused of wasting his possessions. 2 So he called him in and asked him, `What is this I hear about you? Give an account of your management, because you cannot be manager any longer.' 3 "The manager said to himself, `What shall I do now? My master is taking away my job. I'm not strong enough to dig, and I'm ashamed to beg— 4 I know what I'll do so that, when I lose my job here, people will welcome me into their houses.' 5 "So he called in

> each one of his master's debtors. He asked the
> first, `How much do you owe my master?' 6 "
> `Eight hundred gallons of olive oil,' he replied.
> "The manager told him, `Take your bill, sit
> down quickly, and make it four hundred.' 7
> "Then he asked the second, `And how much
> do you owe?' " `A thousand bushels of wheat,'
> he replied. "He told him, `Take your bill and
> make it eight hundred.' 8 "The master com-
> mended the dishonest manager because he
> had acted shrewdly. For the people of this
> world are more shrewd in dealing with their
> own kind than are the people of the light.

Now God can call us into His office anytime He wants and
ask for an accounting, just like this man did of his steward in
Luke 16:2. He could say, "Word on the street is that you've
been wasting my provision. Word on the street is that you've
been acting like you are the boss because I haven't been here
for a while." And so he tells his steward in Luke 16:2 to give
an account of his stewardship. As a matter of fact, the rich man
declares the steward can no longer serve him.

Now digging was a low form of work (verse 3), a hard, hard,
way to make a living. It would be like moving from a nice office
job in an air-conditioned office, to a construction job outside
in the middle of the summer. The steward said, "I just can't do
that!" He was also too ashamed to beg.

So he said, "I've got to do something." Verse 4 reveals his
strategy – he resolved to make some moves that would allow
his master's debtors to receive him once he had been removed
from his job. What he does (and his lord's characterization of
it in verse 8) make this a very interesting parable to interpret.

Why? Because you see that the steward cuts down one of his master's receivables from 100 measures of oil to 50 and another receivable from 100 measures of wheat to 80.

How did the master respond? "The master *commended* the unjust steward, because he had done wisely" *(emphasis mine)*. Huh? We are not used to hearing commendation for somebody who is referred to as unjust. However, we can learn a lesson from somebody who recognizes a bad situation and does something about it. He was dishonest, yes, but he is commended for being shrewd. Jesus said the children of the world operate with shrewdness and the children of light (that's us) would be wise to do so as well (v. 8).

This brings us to our second point about stewardship: not only is stewardship a truth, *stewardship is a trust*. In other words, *use it don't waste it*—with *it* being what you have been given.

Three Wise Actions by One Shrewd Man

This will lead to true wisdom. This steward was getting fired. However, he did three things that you and I would be wise to do.

The first thing he did is *he looked ahead*. That shows anticipation. Many of us don't think to look ahead. We are so busy with the here and now, focusing on our current situation, that we don't take the opportunity to look ahead. This steward said to himself, "What shall I do?" Are you going to ask that question when it comes to your finances? When it comes to your time? When it comes to the relationships you maintain? You have to be able to pause long enough to view the road to see where you are headed.

The second thing he did was *he planned ahead*. That shows application.

He knew he could not dig and he did not want to beg so he decided to reduce the debts of those who owed his master. He thought that when he was out of a job he could find a welcome in their homes because he had affected their pockets in a positive way.

The third thing the steward did was *he actually moved ahead*. That shows action.

Many of us get stuck before completing all three steps. Some never even look ahead. Others at least look ahead, and even start to plan a strategy but then they never actually do anything about it. This steward did all three and that's what makes him a commendable steward.

Do you have any kind of plan for giving? Do you have any kind of plan (or even a thought) about how to deal with your debt? Do you have any plans when it comes to savings or taxes? What about consumption? Have you sat down and looked ahead, planned ahead, and then moved ahead based upon the revolutionary, relevant, and real truth of stewardship? If not, you'd better recognize!

My father told me when he was growing up in his generation, particularly in certain evangelical circles, there was a time it was thought to be unspiritual to have things like life insurance or wills. Not because they were attempting to be derelict in their responsibilities, not because they were lazy, or anything of that nature, but they simply believed that if Christ was to be soon coming, why bother with such encumbrances? Why have any long-term plans? Similar thinking was floating around Thessalonica, and it stopped some folks from going to work (see 2 Thessalonians 3:6-15). Paul had to remind the Thessalonians to get back to work and to work until Jesus comes. Until that happens, they were not to sit around idle, because it would cause problems.

Similarly, you must have a plan for the next generation that you are willing to put into action. You also must have a plan for yourself, particularly as it relates to your retirement (if you think that social security is a plan, it's not gonna happen!) And *no*, the lottery ticket that you're holding in your pocket is *not* a plan. Are you kidding me? That's not even a hope. That's nothing. *You'd better recognize.* You are a steward.

In Luke 16, Jesus is telling us to take a lesson from this steward and ask yourself, "Where am I right now and where am I trying to go?" A commendable steward will *look* ahead, *plan* ahead, and then *move* ahead.

Let's say we've all be trying to arrive at the same location— Sunday worship at New Life Christian Fellowship Church. If you are coming all the way from a distant suburb like Elk Grove, the directions to get to the church are vastly different than if you live around the corner from the church. Now I can help you to get to where you need to be, but you first need to let me know where you are starting. Why? The route will be different based upon your specific location.

The same is true for the destination of financial responsibility. You have to assess your situation like a steward and know exactly where you are – then you can get the directions you need to get to where you need to go. I don't care if you're in debt up to your eyeballs. There's a plan that you can make and undertake right now that will speak to your situation. If you are in a place where you have no debt, you pay your taxes on time and you've got a surplus of cash built up, you may conclude that you have enough so maybe you can aspire to be a double or a triple tither, to honor God. If you've been saving 10% or 15% through your 401k program or a self-directed IRA, if you have your life insurance in a trust, and you have a will completed, then the directions to get to the place that you need to be as a faithful and good steward will be different than somebody who is living check to check with a spotty credit report.

But there is a prescription for you no matter what your situation. And you can get to the place of financial responsibility sooner rather than later. How? You must look ahead, plan ahead, and then move ahead.

In verse 9 Jesus says,

I tell you, use worldly wealth to gain friends for yourselves, so that when it is gone, you will be welcomed into eternal dwellings.

What is he talking about? He's saying stewardship is a trust and the true wisdom of stewardship is you should use what you are given, don't waste it. How do you use it? Make friends for yourself because the wealth will eventually be gone. You may say, "I'm not going to lose my money." My response would be to ask if you know the difference between a burial suit and a regular suit. The answer is burial suits do not have pockets. There is no need for pockets in a burial suit because *you can't take it with you*.

At some point you are going to lose your money. It's not yours anyway—it's just loaned to you, for 70 or 80 years, and then it's going to somebody else! First to the government, and then whatever's left to whoever are your heirs. So, you have to use it while you're here.

Jesus said use it to make friends for yourselves, that you might be welcome into eternal dwellings. He's actually saying to use you time and money in the best places you can – invest it in the kingdom and the people that are going to be in the kingdom. These are the best investments you'll ever make

Imagine this scene in glory: somebody comes up to you who you have never seen or met and they tell you that they are there because of you. You look confused but they tell you to think back to the financial support you gave through your church for a particular ministry or missionary. That missionary preached the gospel to them and they accepted Jesus Christ as personal savior! That person just wanted to thank you because you got in on what God did in their life. Now imagine that scene is repeated over and over again. How awesome that would be!!

The money you give to support the gospel is sown into the kingdom where you and I get the opportunity to build up treasure and fruit for eternity. It is truly the best investment you can ever make – an investment in people. Matthew 6:19-20 reminds us, the treasure on earth will not last. It will get rusty and moldy. Jesus urged his followers,

> **19 "Do not store up for yourselves treasures on earth, where moth and rust destroy, and where thieves break in and steal. 20 But store up for yourselves treasures in heaven, where moth and rust do not destroy, and where thieves do not break in and steal.**

Our possessions are both transitory and ephemeral. But what is lasting, and everlasting, is the treasure that we build up for the kingdom. Therefore, use your wealth, don't waste it.

Let's look at Luke 16 again, verses 10-12, we discover a third point about stewardship. *Stewardship is a test.* In other words, use it, don't abuse it. This will lead to true riches. You didn't know? *You'd better recognize.* Why did God choose money as a test of our character? I don't know. He could have made it something else, but He made it money because we obsess about money and we worry about it constantly. If only we spent as much time focusing on the advancement of the kingdom and the work of the kingdom, as we do worrying about resources. We think about things like, how am I going to pay all of these bills, what trip are we're going to take this year or how I'm going to pay for all of these Christmas gifts. We're always worried about that stuff.

The Stewardship Test

As we look more closely at verses 10-12 we understand more fully that stewardship is a test. Those verses say:

> **10 "Whoever can be trusted with very little can also be trusted with much, and whoever is dishonest with very little will also be dishonest with much. 11 So if you have not been trustworthy in handling worldly wealth, who will trust you with *true riches*? 12 And if you have not been trustworthy with someone else's property, who will give you property of your own?** (*emphasis mine)*

I thought we were already talking about true riches? No, we were talking about money. The material is symbolic of the spiritual. Jesus is revealing that if you can't be trusted with this simple test of money, you're not going to be able to be trusted with the true riches. The true riches are the *kingdom* riches. The true riches are the riches of relationship (with Him and others in the body of Christ), and the riches that come with building and advancing the kingdom and laying up treasure in heaven forever. God wants you to understand that you have to honor Him with your money and with your resources and be faithful with a little.

A History Lesson with Pharaoh

This is a matter of your priorities. Does God come first in your priorities? Believe it or not, Pharaoh tested the priorities of Moses and the children of Israel when Moses sought to lead God's people out of Egypt. Pharaoh hoped to compromise their commitment.

The first compromise is recorded in Exodus 8:25: And Pharaoh called for Moses and for Aaron, and said, ""Go, sacrifice to your God here in the land." Pharaoh said if you have to sacrifice to your God, just do it right here. That offer was designed to be a *compromise on their response to God*. Pharaoh was telling Moses, "Go ahead, sacrifice, just don't actually leave the area and our society." A lot of people still follow the advice of Pharaoh. They worship God exactly where they are. They don't move or change anything. They don't come to know Jesus Christ and there is no transformation or rebirth. They simply put all the trappings of religion around them (prayers, church attendance, good works, etc..). They live according to the society.

That's the *trap of religion*, and it's the first compromise that Pharaoh threw at the children of Israel. The second compromise is designed to make them *compromise on their relationship with God* and is recorded in Exodus 8:27-28:

We must take a three-day journey into the desert to offer sacrifices to the LORD our

> **God, as he commands us." Pharaoh said, "I
> will let you go to offer sacrifices to the LORD
> your God in the desert, but you must not go
> very far. Now pray for me."**

Pharaoh told Moses, "Go, just don't go too far" (only to
the Egyptian suburbs). That's the *trap of recreation*. Satan's
always looking for recreational Christians, not revolutionary
Christians. Satan says, "If you are already a believer I can't
do anything about your salvation, but that 'sanctification pursuit,'—seeking to become more like Christ—I can discourage.
If you have given your life to Christ, Satan wants you to do
nothing with your salvation. Go, but don't go far. Recreational
Christians who profess one thing but do another are still very
useful tools to the enemy.

Pharaoh offered a third compromise to the children of Israel.
Behind this temptation is *the trap of relaxation*:

> **⁸ Then Moses and Aaron were brought back
> to Pharaoh. "Go, worship the LORD your
> God," he said. "But just who will be going?" ⁹
> Moses answered, "We will go with our young
> and old, with our sons and daughters, and
> with our flocks and herds, because we are to
> celebrate a festival to the LORD." ¹⁰ Pharaoh
> said, "The LORD be with you—if I let you go,
> along with your women and children! Clearly
> you are bent on evil. ¹¹ No! Have only the men
> go; and worship the LORD, since that's what
> you have been asking for." Then Moses and
> Aaron were driven out of Pharaoh's presence.
> (Exodus 10:8-11)**

Pharaoh tells Moses that all the men can go but they must leave the women and children behind. That offer is designed to *compromise on their reach for God.* If Pharaoh were approaching us today he would say, "Ok, I understand you are saved, and even being sanctified but you really need to leave the rest of your family with me!"

The Enemy would love to convince you to just relax. Don't share your faith in Christ with those around you. Definitely don't be "on fire" for Jesus. Sit back and relax. Everybody is going to get tired of you soon anyway so try not to bother them (never mind that there are lives at stake!). A relaxed Christian is all right with the Enemy.

The fourth compromise is really Pharaoh's last stand. In Exodus 10:24 it says:

> **Then Pharaoh summoned Moses and said, "Go, worship the LORD. Even your women and children may go with you; only leave your flocks and herds behind."**

This final offer was a *compromise on their resources in God.* This is *the trap of robbery*, withholding what rightly belongs to God. Today Satan tries to spring the trap of robbery. He recognizes he can't stop you from being a Christian and knows you want to take your faith seriously in terms of growth and maturity. You also seem determined to share your faith with those around you. The only thing left to do is see if he can convince you to leave your *wealth* in Egypt. "Leave your checkbook here with me," he urges. Why? Because if you leave your money here, he figures you will be back. And if he can get you to spend more time in Egypt (or the society he provides), then maybe you won't be such a serious Christian after all.

That's the trap of robbery. Moses didn't fall for this compromise because in verse 26 he tells Pharaoh that not a hoof is to be left behind. He told Pharaoh they were taking *everybody* and *everything*. See, when God wants to deliver you often the last thing to come out is your money. You say to God, "I'm with you. I know I need to get saved and I'm out of Egypt. I know I need to move forward and grow and I know I need to grab my family and bring them with me." Then God says to you, "Don't forget your checkbook."

"Wow, I need to take that with me, too?" you reply. "I thought I'd leave that in Egypt."

Your checkbook might need to get delivered today! Moses told Pharaoh to let his people go, and now God is saying to let my people's checkbooks go! But he's not saying that to Pharaoh—He's saying it to you. This is about priority and order in your life, and your willingness to honor God in all that you do. God doesn't need your checkbook but He wants you to give it to Him.

The Test—and Task—You Cannot Skip

That's why stewardship is a test. And guess what? You can't drop this class. Whenever the "semester" is over, God is going to look right at the syllabus (the Word of God), and say, I told you this is what you were going to be graded on. Stewardship is a test so use money and don't abuse it.

And finally, we need to understand that *stewardship is a task*. In other words, *use it, don't serve it.* Luke 16:12 says,

And if you have not been trustworthy with someone else's property, who will give you property of your own?

This verse reminds us that we have to be faithful handling God's affairs first, because that's what a steward is called to do. Luke 16:13 continues:

"No servant can serve two masters. Either he will hate the one and love the other, or he will be devoted to the one and despise the other. You cannot serve both God and Money."

Money makes a great servant. However, it makes a poor master. And if you don't control your money, your money will control you. And that's what it means to love one or the other. If you're a steward, you understand that you have a master, and He's in heaven. If you're a steward you understand that you don't own anything and you've signed a quit claim deed to prove it. Since it is no longer yours, you're not consumed with it.

Now there's nothing wrong with money. As a matter of fact, there's nothing wrong with being affluent, as many people in the Bible like Solomon, Abraham, and Job, were affluent. So are we to conclude that those who have money are trustworthy and righteous and those that don't are not? Not at all. That is the same erroneous thinking that lead the disciples to make the statement "Who then can be saved?" in Matthew 19:25 concerning the rich young man who turned away from Jesus. If the rich man can't get into heaven, who can get there? He's got it made, he has money. Many believed that having worldly resources was proof that you also had the favor of God and were living right before God. Of course, that is an oversimplification. Remember our syllabus is really thick. We've got a whole lot of assignments, and a whole lot of handouts to go over so please don't draw a direct line from money to righteousness.

Money is a test. And what you do with whatever you have is what God will hold you accountable for. If you handle your business with a little, the Scripture says God will give you more to handle on his behalf. But you need the right perspective. Stewardship is a task. Use your money, don't serve it. This will lead to true service. Money is to be used. Again, it can be a great servant for you, but it will always be a poor master.

In Deuteronomy chapter 14:23, it says:

> **Eat the tithe of your grain, new wine and oil, and the firstborn of your herds and flocks in the presence of the LORD your God at the place he will choose as a dwelling for his Name, so that you may learn to revere the LORD your God always.**

Why honor God with your resources? So that you can learn to fear God. That's why He desires a tithe of 10 percent. Why did he say 10 percent? I don't know; He could have said 20 percent or 50 percent. But He said 10 percent and apparently that is enough for you to show your appreciation for what He has provided and to honor Him. Now you must realize that this stewardship concept does not just apply to your money, or *treasure*, but also to your skills, talent and time. There is also stewardship as it relates to the environment and your personal relationships. Truly stewardship applies to everything we have and everything we do (see chapter 5 for more on tithing).

Watch out, though. The Scriptures warn that our money can be a snare. Paul writes:

> **9 People who want to get rich fall into temptation and a trap and into many foolish and**

harmful desires that plunge men into ruin and destruction. 10 For the love of money is a root of all kinds of evil. Some people, eager for money, have wandered from the faith and pierced themselves with many griefs. (1 Timothy 6:9–10)

If you *love* money, you are going to have a problem. Simply because the more you have, the harder it is not to fall in love with it. The harder it is not to try to "keep up with the Joneses." If you don't have the right perspective on money, whether you have a little or a lot, you will always be thinking *more . . . more . . . more*, and it will never be enough. Some even play this game with God. Some will say, "Lord, if you give me more, then, I'll honor you more." STOP—It does not work that way. His response will be, "Why would I give you more, if you don't honor Me with what you have? *You go first*. I can and will take care of you, and you can claim my promises. My promises are right here in the syllabus [*the Bible*]." There are many promises, but there are also premises before the promises. In order to claim the promises, you need to understand the premises. Stewardship is one of those premises. You'd better recognize!

Discussion Questions

1. Stewardship is a truth that is revolutionary, relevant, and real. Has this concept already begun to revolutionize your living? How?
2. The steward in Luke 16 demonstrates that stewardship is a trust. What three things did he do to enable this trust? Are you doing these things?

3. Stewardship is a test in what ways? What could you be willing to compromise on, according to Exodus 8?
4. Stewardship is a task. What is the difference between using money and serving money in our lives?

CHAPTER 3:
I'M JUST WAITING TO EXHALE

With the title, "I'm Just Waiting to Exhale," you might think I'm talking about something else right now — waiting to be able to breathe in a relationship, for example. That's the premise in Terri McMillan's book and movie *Waiting to Exhale*.

In the film the four main characters talk about a time when things would be set right in terms of relationship. They were waiting for a place where each could finally relax and be in a fulfilling relationship with a man. At that point they could literally breathe a sigh of relief. Until then, they were waiting to exhale.

Now, many of us have at one point in our adult lives have been waiting to exhale as it relates not to a relationship but to our *financial situation*. Many of us have said to ourselves, "I wish there could come a day, where I didn't have to sing the song, 'I owe, I owe, it's off to work I go!'" We are waiting for the day when things will be made right in our financial situations. I would argue that you and I do not need to long for a place where we can finally exhale. We need to be *willing to exhale* right where we are, right now. Yet many of us have continually promised God that we will start to make some financial changes once we get to a certain level or once we "get it together." So again, we stumble upon the subject of stewardship.

Now let's drill down to talk specifically about the five areas of our finances to which we must give attention. The first is *debt*, the second is *giving*, the third is *savings*, the fourth is *taxes* and the fifth is *consumption*. Most believers, (well, most people in general, but we're just talking about believers here) don't have any kind of plan for those five areas.

Major portions of the book of Proverbs were written by King Solomon, who was very wealthy and also very wise. That's a great combination! So, when he starts to talk about money, which he does quite a bit in Proverbs, we should pay attention. What is interesting is that many of us don't listen to someone who has their financial situation together. Why? Because, we say, "They can't understand what I'm going through, they are not facing any money troubles." Conversely, when someone doesn't have their money situation in order, we don't listen to them either. Why? Because they can't tell us anything, their finances are just as messed up as ours!

So we find ourselves in a place where we really don't listen to anybody. But if we're going to listen to anybody, I would suggest that we listen to the Lord as He revealed Himself through His servant King Solomon. In Proverbs 22:7 Solomon tells us something very key:

The rich rule over the poor, and the borrower is servant to the lender.

Let's focus on that last phrase, "The borrower is servant to the lender." As we move to a place where we will be willing to exhale, the first thing to discuss is the topic of debt. You might think debt is a material issue, but I would argue that it is not. *Debt is a spiritual issue.* Why? Because debt expresses the underlying problem that we really have.

Imagine: the more that you owe, you actually become servant to whomever you owe the money. That has implications for us in terms of our freedom of choices, does it not? It also has implications for us in terms of the freedom of our time. Many of us are not freed up to spend time with our families or pursue ministry work in the kingdom because of the choices that we have made concerning our desired standard of living. The bills that we have in place—whether a substantial mortgage, car payments or installment loans on other big purchases (typically all of he above)—require many household to have two parents working, sometimes two or three jobs. We do this so we can pay for the things that we already have. And to further exacerbate the problem, we use credit card debt to live beyond our means and to acquire more things we do not have and think we desperately need. We have truly bought into the "American way of life." The American way is *immediate gratification*. How would you describe it? Here is the underlying pitch by those selling goods and services to consumers:

> *If you want it, get it. Now. Why should you wait? You deserve to get what you want, don't you? You work hard every day so you should at least enjoy some of the fruits of your labor, right? So what if you can't really afford it. We will make it easier for you to get it now and pay for it LATER. So what if you have to pay more, at least you've got it! You don't want to fall behind your friends, colleagues, and neighbors, do you? You are just as good as they are so go out there and spend, spend, spend. We're counting on you!*

What producers of consumables and credit card companies are really counting on is not you but what is lurking inside you–*greed*. That is why I said that debt is a spiritual issue. The use of credit card debt in particular gives life to our greed. What is the spiritual answer to greed? *Contentment*. The less content we are, the more debt we are likely to have.

The Recipe for Honoring God

Now let me give you the money recipe for honoring God with our resources: **0, 10, 20, 30, 40**. It's simple to remember but difficult to implement. However, if you and I will do this as it relates to those five areas that are so important in terms of life balance and financial balance, we will discover that we will honor God when it comes to our financial resources. Remember the five financial areas (debt, giving, savings, taxes, consumption)? Now write down these percentages for allocation to those areas: 0, 10, 20, 30, 40.

0% is our allocation to *debt* in order to **stop greed**.

10% goes to *giving* because we need to **sow to God**.

20% is targeted for *savings/investing* so that we might **save for goals**.

30% is set aside for *taxes*, so we can **support the government**.

40% is left for *consumption* so that we can **satisfy with goods**.

Deuteronomy: "You Shall Not Borrow"

So, let's start with the first percentage, which is zero. That percentage relates to the first area, which is debt. The phrase we will associate with 0 percent debt is "stop greed." And the way that we can stop greed, the way that we can get a handle on our appetites if you will, is to go forward financially with zero percent allocated to debt.

You might be saying to yourself right now, *Man, you're crazy!* Yet I believe God's perspective on debt is summarized in Romans 13:8a, which says, "Owe no man anything, but to love one another." Now I am not trying to pull that verse out of its context, but I do think it is a succinct and accurate statement that reflects God's desire for us in terms of borrowing.

Look also at Deuteronomy 28. After God revealed through Moses all of the laws, ordinances, and statutes, he began to summarize everything by saying that if the children of Israel followed His commands, they would be blessed and if they did not, they would be cursed:

> **1 If you fully obey the LORD your God and carefully follow all his commands I give you today, the LORD your God will set you high above all the nations on earth. 12 The LORD will open the heavens, the storehouse of his bounty, to send rain on your land in season and to bless all the work of your hands. You will lend to many nations but will borrow from none. 13 The LORD will make you the head, not the tail. If you pay attention to the commands of the LORD your God that I give you this day and carefully follow them, you**

will always be at the top, never at the bottom. (v.1,12-13)

Clearly one of the blessings of obedience was that the children of Israel would be lenders and not borrowers. Now look later in Deuteronomy 28 to see the converse if they did not obey the Lord:

> **[43]The alien who lives among you will rise above you higher and higher, but you will sink lower and lower. [44] He will lend to you, but you will not lend to him. He will be the head, but you will be the tail.**

Interestingly enough, you should be able to glean a little bit about the state of the Children of Israel by looking at whether or not they were borrowing or lending.

No Debt, Except . . .

I know what I am telling you is hard to hear right now because you are thinking about all of your debt. You should be. "Owe no man . . .but to love." Zero percent to debt. We should not accrue debt. This is the goal and the point at which we need to arrive. Now, of course, there are a couple of exceptions to this mandate. Debt is acceptable, but only under certain circumstances.

. . . Secured Debt

The first exception *(speaking specifically)* is *secured debt*. What is secured debt? It is debt that is secured by an asset, hopefully one that is appreciating in value. For example, if you have taken out a mortgage on your home, that debt is secured by your residence. If that debt were immediately due or you could no longer afford the mortgage payments due to a change in circumstances, you would have the necessary means to repay the loan by selling the asset (assuming the house is worth more than the loan).

Remember that automobiles are *depreciating* assets. You can buy a car on credit because it is secured by the value of the vehicle. But the value of the car depreciates year by year, so the level of debt associated with its purchase should be at a much lower level than a home purchase—and it almost always is. However, an identified source of repayment is the first hurdle towards us answering the question, "Can I afford to do this?" Secured debt helps jump that hurdle because it confirms that it can be done.

The next hurdle is much more involved because it deals not with "*Can* I do this?" but "*Should* I do this?" The 0, 10, 20, 30, 40 money recipe helps us to align our finances rightly so that the second hurdle can be appropriately addressed. The problem with unsecured debt is that there is no identified source of repayment at the time of purchase. Since there is none, we should wait until there is. We should have the resources on hand; otherwise we are simply living above and beyond our means. It becomes a spiritual standoff between our fleshly desire—which can become greed—and our spiritual require-ment— to be content. Greed says, "Consume now and give no thought to how or how much you will have to pay tomorrow." Contentment says, "I will wait until I can truly afford this pur-chase by answering the questions, "Can I do this?" and "Should I do this?" *If I cannot say yes to both then I don't need it.*"

. . . Debt That Yields an Income

The second exception to the 0 percent debt requirement is *debt related to an income-producing investment*. For example, let's say you are able to buy a piece of real estate for $100,000 and you will receive $10,000 in net proceeds a year. So the return will be 10 percent ($10,000 divided by $100,000). Now, assume that you hold this asset for ten years (receiving your $10,000 per year every year) and then you sold it for $100,000, which is what you paid for it. Your annual rate of return over the ten-year holding period remains 10 percent.

That's what is called an unleveraged return, because no debt was involved. See, financial people don't call borrowed money debt; they call it *leverage*. (Sounds more sophisticated, huh?)

Now let's put some *leverage* on this asset. Let's imagine that we can borrow 75 percent of the money (that's $75,000) at an 8 percent interest rate (interest only). Every year we receive our $10,000, we need to use $6,000 to pay the mortgage interest ($75,000 x 8 percent) and we get to keep the rest, which is $4,000. So now our return has increased because we have only invested $25,000 of our own money (we borrowed the other $75,000 we needed) and every year after we pay our $6,000 mortgage payment, we get to keep $4,000. Our leveraged return is now 16 percent ($4,000/$25,000), which is higher than the unleveraged return of only 10 percent. That's called positive leverage. If we can find three more investments just like this one, we can put all of our $100,000 to work and get a 16 percent return with debt instead of just a 10 percent return in one asset without debt.

We must be very careful, though, because we're taking risk to achieve those returns. You need to underwrite or evaluate the underlying asset. If the property were an office building and you had a Fortune 500 company as the tenant occupying your space, you could feel pretty good about actually receiving that return. If you had a retail property with a start-up restaurant with limited capital as a tenant, the likelihood that you will get your 10 percent for the next ten years decreases greatly. In that case, you'd better be prepared to be able to pay the mortgage off. Part of that preparation is making sure you understand the value of the building with no income-producing tenant.

. . . Educational Debt

The third exception to the 0 percent debt requirement relates is *educational debt*. Investing in your education through student loans is a worthwhile pursuit. The identified source of repayment at the time of borrowing is *you* and the vocational opportunity— an income generating job—you should be able to secure with a quality education. The repayment does not start until after graduation with the assumption that employment will have begun. What is the risk? First and foremost it is you. You must be disciplined, diligent and focused while you are in school in order to put yourself in the best position to reap the benefits of this investment. There is also the risk that the professional field that you have chosen to pursue may not have sufficient opportunity for graduates of your institution. Many trade schools and non-traditional four-year colleges/universities are very willing to take your money but do not have the wherewithal to connect the majority of their graduates to sustainable careers. Lastly, you should also be circumspect about the level of debt that you accumulate. Greater debt amounts increase the risk of repayment and can also limit your options after graduation. I can recall a few opportunities that I could not pursue upon graduation from college (e.g. certain stockbroker jobs that had much lower initial pay but provided great upside if you were successful) simply because I had student loans that needed to be addressed. The two hurdles of can I do this, and should I do this still apply but educational loans are distinct enough to merit special mention.

Beyond these few exceptions, heed the scriptural warning: **"Owe no man anything."** It's better for your emotional health, it's better for your physical health and it's better for the kingdom, in terms of your time and resources. *Everything* is better when you and I don't have debt. **When looking at your money allocation recipe, you can include these exceptions in your consumption area, and not count them towards your debt.**

Are Credit Cards the Road to Independence?

For many of us the debt trap started in college. At the time "You have been pre-approved" were the most beautiful words I had ever seen. For me, those words came with the Visa Card, they came with MasterCard, and they came with another Visa Card from a different bank.

If you were at college and applied for all the offers at the same time, the card issuers never knew how many cards you had, and you could walk around with three and four credit cards at once. So when you would call home and tell your parents that you needed something and they said "No!", you could scream "Credit means get it!" and not have to wait for anything.

That is where many of us started to get into some bad patterns. We used credit cards to get some financial independence from our parents, and we used it to live beyond our means because we were not content with where we were. It is the same situation today.

Can We Learn to Be Content?

Can we learn to be content? The apostle Paul wrote, "But godliness with contentment is great gain. For we brought nothing into this world, and it is certain we can carry nothing out. And having food and raiment let us be therewith content."

You can be godly and not be content. However, Paul says that if you can get some contentment as part of your godliness, that's a great gain. You come into this world with nothing and you will definitely leave with nothing. Therefore, you need to be content with what you do have. When you and I get to a place where we are not content, we expose ourselves to all manner of ruin and destruction (1 Timothy 6:9). And if you don't believe me, look back at some point in your life, and see the ruin and destruction that follows our greed. Pull out your credit report. Look at your history, particularly when you were living well beyond your means and your debt was drowning you. Recall your relationships, your health, and your commitment to kingdom pursuits at that time. Your debt probably was causing you all manner of problems, stress, and strain.

Let's Meet at the Watering Hole

The way we think about money reminds me of the African watering hole. When the water is high, during the rainy season, everybody drinks. Zebras, gazelles, giraffes, even little birds. Everybody is welcome to come get something to drink because there is plenty of water. But what happens when the water runs dry? When the water runs dry, only the biggest and the strongest—only those that can push their weight around at the hole—can drink. Everybody else starts fighting over the little that remains, and it is a time of great conflict and stress. The herds start to thin out and many start to die.

We seem to approach our money matters as if the water is never going to run out. We look at what our situation is right now and say, "This is great and the water is high in the watering hole right now." So, we never prepare for when the water gets low. We max everything out. Later, if one thing goes wrong, you have one little hiccup, it immediately becomes a time of great crisis and stress. That's what is meant by "living check to check." Most folks I know are living that way; if they miss their next paycheck, it's over. That means that if some of the water leaves the watering hole, they have no other supply.

Oh, but we *do* have a supply. And there are some promises that we can tap into, but we must live right, in order to access these promises. See, there's always a premise before the promise. And if we are not living the premise, if we're not applying the principle, then we really don't have a right to claim the promise.

The Secret to Paul's Success

In Philippians 4:10–13, Paul shares with us one little principle. This principle happens to be the secret to the apostle's success. Paul was excited about his relationship with the Philippian church, and this letter was partly a thank-you for the contributions they had made to him in the ministry. He was in need and they came to his assistance as they had opportunity. Yet he had learned to be content. He says:

> **10 I rejoice greatly in the Lord that at last you have renewed your concern for me. Indeed, you have been concerned, but you had no**

> **opportunity to show it. [11] I am not saying
> this because I am in need, for I have learned
> to be *content* whatever the circumstances.
> (*emphasis mine*)**

That contentment sustains him even when he was in need of food. He continues:

> **[12] I know what it is to be in need, and I know
> what it is to have plenty. I have learned the
> secret of being content in any and every sit-
> uation, whether well fed or hungry, whether
> living in plenty or in want.**

Paul is saying, "I know how it is when the water runs dry, and in that situation, I've been all right. I also know how it is when everything is flowing, when there is money, and there are resources, and everything is going well. I know how it is when you just receive a job promotion because I've been there. I know how to eat steak and lobster and I also know how to survive when all I have is a bag of noodles. I know the difference between the two because I've been there, done that."

Now he declares the secret:

> **[13] I can do everything through him who gives
> me strength.**

That's the secret to contentment. That's the secret to success. That's the secret to life, to know and understand that you can do all things through Christ who gives you strength.

The truth is Paul was *dependently independent*. You and I need to get to a place where we know and understand that we are dependently independent. Paul statement did not emanate from some kind of stoic philosophy that says, "I'll be all right, because I've prepared for myself, and I can take care of myself." Paul is saying that he is indeed independent, but the reason is because he is dependent on Christ! He gets what he needs *from* Christ, and he can do all things *through* Christ who gives him strength. That's how Paul could be down yet feel up. That's how he could deal with being well fed and hungry. That is also why he could conclude his thoughts with a promise in verse 19:

19 And my God will meet all your needs according to his glorious riches in Christ Jesus.

God gives to those He is in relationship with according to his riches in glory. That's the final part of the secret. Governing our lives by this secret will allow us to experience lives filled with contentment. We have to stop waiting to exhale, and be willing to exhale right here, right now. We have to stop making these dangerous presumptions about what's going to happen in the future as it relates to our resources, and start preparing ourselves to honor God with our resources in the present.

How to Know You Have a Debt Problem

How can you tell if you have a debt problem? Here's the first sign: *You're living on credit instead of on cash*. If that's the case, you might have a debt problem. How do you know? The balance keeps going up. You also might be using one credit card to pay off another credit card. If so, you may have a debt problem.

This is really about contentment. I *want* it now, but I know I can't *afford* it now, but the bank says I can *get* it now, so I

55

go ahead and *buy* it now. The latest clothes and shoes? It's the least I can do for myself. How do I pay for it later? Not worried about it today!

The second sign of a debt problem is that *you constantly pay the minimum on your credit cards*. You pay the minimum because that's all you can afford. Of course, with the 18 percent (or higher) annual interest, your balance continues to increase even when you make fewer purchases.

Here's a third sign of a likely debt problem: *you are unable to save, tithe, or even pay your taxes*. If you cannot do any of those things, excessive debt is probably the culprit. We as a society have a debt problem and we as individuals have debt problems because we live beyond our means. We make outsized purchases, because we're always trying to "front" and "floss."

That's just the way we do it. The comedian Chris Rock talked about that. He mentioned that people (particularly black people since he is most familiar with his own group) spend their money like it's going to rot if they don't. We seem to love flash, and we love to put everything that we have, everything that we own, on our backs (clothes) and in the driveways of our houses or apartments (cars). That's because we're always trying to impress somebody—somebody I would argue who doesn't even like us, and who we don't even really know!

"Get It Now!"

Let me tell you, there is nothing easy about easy payments. All thirty-six of those payments will be hard. Especially if they are charging you 15 percent interest. Let me give you an example. You just signed the lease on a new apartment, and you want to have your family come over and celebrate with you.

In other words, "Momma and them" are coming over. And it's not Momma that's really the issue. It's "and them." They are coming over too. And you say to yourself, "I have to get some furniture in here." And so you go down to the furniture store and you buy $5,000 worth of furniture, basically because your family is coming over. That's why you did it, because you want to have everything in order, and you want it when? Now! You can't possibly tell your family that you don't have money for furniture right now and that you plan to save up for it. You can't tell your *loved* ones that you will let them know when you get some furniture but in the meantime bring a folding chair with you because your party is BYOC (bring your own chair). No, you can't do that because then everybody is going to know that you don't have anything and that you barely got this apartment. But you know what? *That's okay.*

So many times you and I are concerned with what everybody else thinks that we buy into the myopic view of the world, which says "Get it now." This goes along with getting something in the mail that says "pre-approved." You say, "Great, I have been pre-approved, so that must mean I am special. This is a prestigious, limited-time offer. I'm in a privileged group. Look at me, I'm pre-approved! It's really simple. All you have to do is call the toll-free number, give your name, and your validation code, and you'll receive your new credit card. Now you can toddle on down to the furniture store and buy $5,000 worth of furniture . . .at 15 percent interest.

Just Pay $100 a month and . . .

Why would you do that? Because even though you know you can't afford to pay $5,000, you *think* you can afford the minimum credit card payment per month. The minimum monthly payment is 2 percent of the balance, which is $100. That's not a lot, you say, but how long will it take you to pay that off that furniture at $100 each month? It will take you seventy-nine months, which is a little less than seven years. "Just" six years and seven months to pay off that furniture. But in the very first month you are paying $62.50 dollars, for just interest.

You're barely whittling down the outstanding balance. Now imagine that instead of buying furniture on credit, you opened up a money market account and earned 5percent annual interest. Once you open that money market account, guess what you are? You're a lender, not a borrower (Deuteronomy 28:12). The bank is paying you, you're not paying the bank. Now here's the interesting part. If you could put $100 dollars a month away (in your money market account at 5 percent annual interest) for the next forty-six months, you could walk into the store, and *pay cash* for that furniture.

"Wow, but I would have to wait almost four years to get it!" you say. Yes, you would have to *wait!* Now ask yourself, what is the real opportunity cost to you at the end of 79 months of waiting or not waiting to buy that furniture? If you wait and delay your gratification by paying with cash, you will get your furniture in month forty-six and then you can take that same $100 dollars and continue to invest it over the next thirty-three months. If you don't wait, at the end of 79 months all you have is furniture. If you wait, at the end of the 79 months you've got the furniture (newer I might add) *and* you have $3,500 in the bank! That's the real cost of getting it now. It's the $3,500 you forgo at the end of that time.

But you did not want to wait. That is the sickness and loss associated with debt. That is why we have to avoid it. And the next time your furniture wears out, if you just kept investing the same $100 a month, you could walk in and pay cash again and get what you need. Just keep going with your $100 a month program, and you will be a lender, and not a borrower. If we are patient, good things (even cash money things) will come. If you and I live above our means, we will live with debt. And if you're a good steward, it's hard to justify doing that. It's hard to justify giving away your hard-earned money on interest payments just to get something now.

The Final Sign of a Debt Problem

The fourth sign of a debt problem (or that your finances are in disarray) is *you gravitate toward "get rich quick" ideas*. Let me tell you something that you really know but choose to ignore: *If it sounds too good to be true, it is.* You're being set up! I guess the part that bothers me the most about these kinds of schemes (and that's what they are) is that those who run them exploit the desperation of people that are already dealing with financial strain in their life.

The more financial strain that you have, the more vulnerable you are to try to get something for nothing. It doesn't happen, and it never works. The best way you can get something for nothing, is have a rich relative pass away and leave it to you. Now that's the American way to get rich! Unless you have that situation coming in the near future, then you need to have a better plan. And a get-rich-quick scheme is not a plan. It's not. If you can make 800 percent on your money in three days, it's a scam. If the opportunity requires you to do nothing or requires no skill or expertise, yet you are told you'll make a great deal of money, your desperation is being exploited.

Remember that you did not get into debt overnight so you're not going to get out of debt overnight. And anybody who tells you that you can is lying to you. You might as well go to Las

Vegas and sit at the blackjack table because you're gambling. If you give somebody your money because they have promised you something that sounds too good to be true, as Malcolm X would say, "You've been had. You've been took. You've been hoodwinked. Bamboozled. Led astray. Run amok!" And many of us can look back and reflect at the times that we tried to get something for nothing, and it never, **ever** works out.

Going into Debt Is Like Snorkeling

Going into debt, is like snorkeling in the ocean. You get offshore a little bit, and you put your head down in the water and you start to look at the fish and it's wonderful. However, because you are distracted by the coral formations and the colorful fish, you don't realize that the current is taking you away from the shore. By the time you stop and look up, you're so far away from the shore that you exclaim in a panic, "How did I get way out here?! Where is the shore?!"

That's how debt creeps up on you. There are not necessarily huge movements that push you into the ocean of debt, but a steady slow current that causes you to drift where you did not plan to go.

If Debt Is Pulling You into the Deep:
Five Solutions

There are five things that I want to recommend that you do if debt is pulling —or has pulled—you into the deep.

First, you need to *seek forgiveness*. Remember, our spending is a spiritual thing. You need to sit down and talk with God. You might say,

"As I look at my life circumstances, especially my financial situation, I realize that I have not been content. I have lived beyond my means and my credit report reflects that. The great strain that I'm feeling concerning my finances and all of the anxiety that I have is my doing because it is based upon the choices I have made. But now that I have been reminded that I know better, I am going to do better. Forgive me Lord for my shortcomings in this area and help me to please you with my finances."

You may ask, "Why would I need to ask forgiveness? Doesn't that seem a little dramatic?" You should seek forgiveness because God is not pleased if you are in a place where you are unable to tithe or unable to save or unable to pay your taxes. Something is out of balance in terms of your financial picture, and you need to talk to the Lord and confess your shortcoming to Him and let Him know you want to do better. Instead of 0 percent debt, 10 percent giving, 20 percent savings, 30 percent taxes, and 40 percent consumption, maybe you have a 40 percent debt allocation, with nothing towards giving and savings. (For the most part, you will always have some tax allocation since the government likes to get paid up front. However, you can operate in such a way that at the end of the year you owe more than the amount the government has withheld). The rest of your money you simply allocate toward consumption. Between your credit card debt (representing past consumption not paid for) and your current consumption, you could be allocating over 80 percent of your resources to satisfy all of your desires (wants and needs). That would indicate a spiritual problem—greed. That problem requires a spiritual solution—forgiveness.

The second solution to your problem is to *stop overspending*. Proverbs 21:17 says,

He who loves pleasure will become poor; whoever loves wine and oil will never be rich.

Wine and oil in that Scripture represent the luxuries of life. If you love all of the luxuries of life, your chances of being rich actually fade away. Why? Because you're spending more than you need to be spending and when you do that, you end up with less. And so the practical application of Solomon's wisdom is that if you don't have your spending in check, you're not going to have anything left.

Ecclesiastes 6:9 says,

Better what the eye sees than the roving of the appetite. This too is meaningless, a chasing after the wind.

It is better for you to concentrate on what's right in front of you and consume what is on your plate, than having a wandering appetite for things you can't have. Put another way, our yearnings often outstrip our earnings. However, you need to be content with your plate. Looking around with a great appetite can make you unsatisfied with what you already have and cause you to wander away in pursuit of things you cannot afford

Conclusion? Stop overspending. What does that really mean? No new debt. Sorry, that sounds so practical because it is. You have to make a commitment. If you want to be serious about financial stewardship, you have to ask forgiveness for your appetite. Your appetite is exceeding what God has currently provided, and you need to wait on Him. Be willing to exhale, understanding that your strength and provision lies in Him, and say "I will be content with what I have." If you can say that then the practical application is that you will not incur any new credit card debt.

If you cannot pay for it with cash, don't get it. Hey, what about Christmas time? Again, *if you cannot pay for it with cash, don't get it.* Your kids will be just fine. "But you do not understand, my son wants the new video game system. It only costs $600 (with one controller) but I would have to get the second controller plus a few games, so all in maybe it would be about $750. He's my baby; shouldn't I just go ahead and put that on the credit card?" If you have not saved for it already, then don't get it. *No new debt.* You must make a commitment today. If you never commit to it, you will never do it. What did the steward do? As soon as he recognized that his situation changed, he did three things. He looked ahead, he planned ahead, and he moved ahead. I am telling you right now, look ahead. You know what your financial situation looks like. You know what your cash flow (or lack thereof) situation looks like. So plan ahead —no new debt. Now move ahead and do it. Or, actually *don't* do it. Stop overspending.

The third solution that you need to implement if you are going to straighten out your finances is *start budgeting*. When some people hear the word "budget," it is like somebody has spit in their face and cussed them. They say, "I work every day and there's no way in the world I'm going to be on a budget. A budget is for people that don't have any money." That is true, but it is also for people who have money.

What did Solomon say about the subject in Proverbs 27:23-24? He advised,

**Be sure you know the condition of your flocks,
give careful attention to your herds; 24 for**

**riches do not endure forever, and a crown is
not secure for all generations.**

Solomon warned the people, "You need to know the condition of your herds and your flocks because otherwise you
can look up and find them gone!" The same current we talked
about that can take you out into the ocean of debt, can cause
you to drift away from your assets and possessions. You can
easily look up and wonder how you arrived at a place where all
of your resources are gone. I can tell you how you got to that
place. You never stopped long enough to take account of what
you own and what you owe. That's a budget.

Pause and look at what you are spending. You will be
amazed at what you spend, and what you spend it on. Just take
a month and write down every transaction big and small (I did it
for many years). I mean *everything*. (Give somebody a quarter
for a piece of bubble gum? Write it down). You will find out
how many frivolous and unnecessary purchases that you make.
You will find out what you are spending for gas, clothing, entertainment, transportation, and housing. If you never take stock
of what you spend as Solomon suggests, you will look up and
half your flock will be gone. Start budgeting. Know where your
money is going and live within your means.

In *Your Money Counts,* Howard Dayton has a chapter enti-
tled "Act Your Wage." I love that. Growing up I used to hear
all the time that I needed to act my age. I interpreted Howard
Dayton's encouragement similarly. Do only what your finances
allow you to do. No more. Live within your means. The only
way you're going to know your means is if you can take stock
of what is coming in, what is going out, and what's left.

Maybe you already have a budget. If so, good. However,
let me say this: if you have a budget and God's not in it, you

need to reshape your budget. If you have a budget and savings is not in it, you need to reshape your budget. If you have a budget that shows multiple credit card payments, then you might want to make some changes. Unfortunately, messed up finances indicate a messed up life. That's tough but it's true. It's tight, but it's right. If God is not honored in your finances, the likelihood that God is honored in your life the way that He should be is very slim.

Let me give you an example. If you've been to college you recall that for every class you took, a syllabus was handed out at the beginning of the term. For a particular class the syllabus may indicate that your final grade would be based 25 percent on homework, 30 percent on a midterm exam and 45 percent on the final. Now if you never turn in any of your homework but you absolutely ace the midterm and the final, the highest percentage you can receive is 75 percent. That's a C.

Now imagine a Christian syllabus. Let's allocate 25 percent of your "grade" to giving, 30 percent to sharing and 45 percent to living. That's giving to God, sharing with others and living for Christ. (That's a pretty decent Christian syllabus!) But if you're not honoring God with your finances or being a good steward over your resources, that's the equivalent of wasting that part of your grade. You get a zero on that. Even if you get an 'A' on everything else, the best you can do overall is 75%. So, if you're not doing what you're supposed to do in all areas that God has given you, you can never get more than a 'C' (the way I have outlined it for you, just for illustrative purposes). Do you want to have a 'C' life? Do you want to get sharing right and living right and then get giving wrong? You'll just be an average Christian if you don't excel in all of these things. 0, 10, 20, 30, 40. It all works together, and you can't afford to ignore any of it. If you are not excelling at the giving portion, the likelihood that you're knocking the cover off the ball in the living and sharing areas is again pretty slim. In the same way, if you are not doing all of the homework, the likelihood that you're going to ace the midterm and ace the final is pretty slim.

The fourth solution to your situation is *sacrifice consuming.* Look at these two verses from Proverbs:

The plans of the diligent lead to profit as surely as haste leads to poverty. (21:5)

he who gathers money little by little makes it grow. (13:11b)

These verses remind us that if you just focus on gathering money little by little, and you remain diligent, you will see a difference in the long run. You may say, "I have way too many bills and too many problems." I understand that, but you must start somewhere. If you put all of your income and expenses down on paper, that's a start. You also must decide that you want to move from the place where you currently are, to a place where you honor God with your money. You must decide to move from your current portfolio allocation to one that mirrors 0, 10, 20, 30, 40. However, you must realize you won't get there overnight. It may take you two years, it may take you three years, it may take you five years, but if you don't look ahead, you'll never plan ahead, and if you don't plan ahead, you'll never move ahead.

So look at your income statement and ask yourself, "*Where can I sacrifice some of my consumption?*" Look for areas to cut expenses, and then use the money saved to pay off some of the credit card debt. If you get additional money in the near future, don't run out and consume all of it. No! Do not get another thing that'll be obsolete six months after you buy it. If you want to honor God with your money, you will do something different in terms of how you spend the money you currently have. You *will* cut and sacrifice some of your consumption in order to bring it in line so that you can honor God with your resources. And if you do not do that, you are not serious. If you do not do that, you are not a good steward. If you do not do that, you are not going to get a good grade in this class. Not according to the syllabus. Amen? Oftentimes it is good to target one of your smaller credit card balances regardless of the interest rate being charged (intuitively you would want to pay down the one with the highest interest rate in order to maximize the interest savings). This way you can completely pay off one bill as quickly as possible. It is amazing how encouraging it can be to mail even one less bill each month. Once you conquer one small bill, you are on your way!

Stay the Course

The fifth and final solution you need to enact is to *stay the course*. (Did you just hear George H.W. Bush's voice in your head? – I did!) It's hard to do this, is it not? It's going to be very difficult to do what you need to do. But here is an encouragement from scripture in Galatians 6:9:

> **Let us not become weary in doing good, for at the proper time we will reap a harvest if we do not give up.**

Do not start this process, get discouraged, and then say, "I'm just not making enough progress." Yes you are—if you take it step by step, little by little. Come up with a plan to honor

God and then move on it one step at a time. As a matter of fact, the picture you should get when you think about the process of change is a teacup that has to fill up a barrel. A person takes the teacup, fills it with water, and then empties it in the barrel. It will not seem at first that any progress is being made but if the person just keeps doing it over and over, sooner or later the barrel starts to fill up. Again, you didn't get into this financial twist overnight, and you're not going to get out of it overnight. But we start by changing our hearts to embrace contentment and not pursue greed. Hebrews 13:5-6 says this:

> **5 Keep your lives free from the love of money and be content with what you have, because God has said, "Never will I leave you; never will I forsake you." 6 So we say with confidence, "The Lord is my helper; I will not be afraid. What can man do to me?"**

This Scripture reminds us that we *can* be content because God tells us that He will never leave us or forsake us. In short, God is reassuring us that no matter what's going on, we still have Him! And if you and I have Him, we should be content with that because in Him we have everything we <u>need</u>. If we're walking the way He wants us to walk, we have access to everything He has and He will pour into our lives the things that we need at the right time, in due time and on time. Be content with what you have, for our God will never leave us or forsake us. Exhale.

Discussion Questions:

1. What does greed have to do with debt? What does godliness have to do with contentment?
2. Are there types of debt that are okay? If so, what are these areas? Do you agree that this kind of debt is okay?
3. According to this chapter, there are signs of having a debt problem. Do you have a debt problem, or are you close to having a problem?
4. Look over the five steps at the end of this chapter. Where do you need to start to clear up your debt?

CHAPTER 4:
GIVING FOR A LIVING

How to Allocate Your Money

0% is our allocation to debt in order to stop greed.

10% goes to giving because we need to sow to God.

20% is targeted for savings/investing so that we might save for goals.

30% is set aside for taxes, so we can support the government.

40% is left for consumption so that we can satisfy with goods.

We now turn our focus to the second parameter in our money recipe of 0, 10, 20, 30, 40. Of course we know that the 0% allocation is to debt. This helps us to *stop greed*. Now we're moving to 10%, which relates directly to our financial giving. We are to *sow to God*. But before we get to some of the particulars of the subject, we need to set the foundation by focusing on our key passage, 2 Corinthians 8. Here we see the apostle Paul encouraging the Corinthians based upon events in the church of Macedonia:

> **1 And now, brothers, we want you to know about the *grace* that God has given the Macedonian churches. 2 Out of the most severe trial, their overflowing joy and their extreme poverty welled up in rich gener-osity. 3 For I testify that they gave as much as they were able, and even beyond their**

ability. Entirely on their own, 4 they urgently pleaded with us for the privilege of sharing in this service to the saints. 5 And they did not do as we expected, but they gave themselves first to the Lord and then to us in keeping with God's will. (*emphasis mine*)

There is a unique mind-set that goes along with giving, and the Macedonians clearly had it. If you and I are going to be giving for a living, we need to first and foremost *develop the mind-set of giving*. Look at what kind of mind-set the Macedonians had. It is the mind-set that reflects a positive out-look and a mind-set that relies on Christ. Paul says their trial no more diminished their joy, than their poverty diminished their generosity (verse 2)! That is an interesting parallel. He said they were in severe trial. But when they were faced with this severe trial, Paul said they were overcome with *joy*. And that's how we're supposed to be in our trial. There was severe trial and there was overflowing joy. Paul also tells us they were facing severe poverty, but yet and still, there was overflowing *generosity*.

The Mind-set for Giving

How is that possible? *They had the right mind-set for giving*. It's the mind-set that the apostle Paul describes in Philippians 4:13—the "I can" attitude. Many of us have the mind-set of "I can't." Some of us have the mind set of "it's too much for me." Others have the mind set of "you don't understand my circumstances." The apostle Paul would tell you that the cir-cumstances are irrelevant. What's important is our God, and whether I am set high, or set low, "I can do everything through him who gives me strength" (Philippians 4:13).

So both Macedonian churches, Berea and Philippi, were able to develop the mind-set of "I can" and therefore give in such a way that they could give out of their poverty, as well as their generosity. They were giving for a living.

Giving should be like *breathing* for a believer. It should be something that you don't even think about. You prepared for it, you plan for it, and it is just what you do. In 2 Corinthians 8:3, Paul attests that the Macedonians gave above and beyond their ability.

Giving Is about Sacrifice, Selflessness, Sharing, and Submitting

This was only possible because they understood that *giving is about sacrifice*. That's what King David contemplated when he was planning to build an altar to the Lord. In II Samuel 24, David approached Araunah to buy his threshing floor and Araunah countered by offering to give him the threshing floor, animals to sacrifice, and the necessary wood at no cost (v. 18-25). But David's response was that he would pay for what was needed because he would not sacrifice to God that which cost him nothing! He understood that giving required sacrifice, and sacrifice has to <u>cost</u> something.

Giving also goes hand-in-hand with selflessness. They gave because they heard that there was a need someplace else. They urgently pleaded with Paul to let them be part of what God was doing (verse 4). They didn't have much of anything, but they knew God was at work so they pleaded to help someone else in need.

The Macedonians further understood that *giving is about sharing*. The word "fellowship" in verse 4 is the Greek word *koinonia*. That is a popular Greek word in Christian circles and it connotes fellowship and partnership, despite the circumstances. (Paul speaks about his relationship with the Macedonian believers at Philippi in Philippians 1:5 as a partnership in the gospel using the same Greek word).

Finally, they understood that *giving is about submitting* to the Lord. Some may think it's about God wanting to separate you from your money. Actually, God wants to separate you from yourself! He does not want your money, He does not need your money. He wants what your money represents. In verse 5, Paul says the Macedonian believers did not do as we expected, but they gave themselves, *first to the Lord*. See, that's submission. Anyone that gets in line with God's giving program understands that they're submitting first to God, because that's what God has instructed us to do. Once we submit ourselves to God, He reveals His will to us, and He allows us to get in on what He's doing.

The Macedonians submitted themselves to God and heard from Him. They understood giving is about sharing, sacrifice, and selflessness, but it's mostly about submission. These folks didn't have the mindset that they would come up at the end of a service, after hearing a good sermon, walk up to the offering plate, and say, "We're going to give God a tip. Nice sermon, buddy. Here's a little something for the effort." God doesn't need a tip from you. What God needs is your life. And you and I both know that much of who we are is wrapped up in our planners and our checkbooks. That's because how we spend our time and how we spend our money speaks volumes about who we really are. You and I need to understand that giving is about submitting to God.

The Mandate for Giving

So, these believers had the mind-set of giving. But Paul calls the Corinthian believers to also observe *the mandate for giving*. He writes:

> **So we urged Titus, since he had earlier made a beginning, to bring also to completion this act of *grace* on your part. 7 But just as you excel in everything—in faith, in speech, in knowledge, in complete earnestness and in your love for us—see that you also excel in this *grace* of giving. (vs. 6-7, *emphasis mine*)**

So, once again the "syllabus" of the Christian life requires that we excel in many areas, including giving. The Corinthian church was a very gifted church and excelled in many areas (I Corinthians 1:5-7). But now he reminds them that they needed to excel in the area of giving as well. That's the mandate.

The Motivation for Giving

Next Paul reveals *the motivation for giving*.

> **8 I am not commanding you, but I want to test the sincerity of your love by comparing it with the earnestness of others. 9 For you know the *grace* of our Lord Jesus Christ, that though he was rich, yet for your sakes he became poor, so that you through his poverty might become rich. (vs.8-9, *emphasis mine*).**

The apostle did not want to command them on this (although the mandate was clear). He could have just said, "Do it, because I said so." He could have gone the parent route. But instead he says, "I want to appeal to you, so that you may have the proper motivation for giving". Do you realize that if giving was some sort of insurance policy like some people make it out to be, there would be millions of people in the world that would love to get in on that plan? "All I have to do is give God some of my money and I can get God off my back? Sounds good." I could line up half the unbelievers I know to take that deal because that would truly be an insurance policy (just in case ol' Chris is right about that whole heaven/hell/God thing). That is both an improper and poor motivation.

What about the popular giving motivation of sowing a dollar and getting a hundred dollars back? Who would not want that deal? Those that trumpet that "truth" are usually the same ones that would entice us by telling us giving is all that matters. They would say "Don't worry about the meaning, don't worry about the motivation. Don't worry about spiritual growth and maturity. Just write the check." That's *not* how God does things. If He did that, it would mean that you and I could drink and smoke, lead loose lifestyles, gamble, cheat on our spouses, abuse our kids and do all other kinds of things as long as we gave enough money to our church. Sorry, that's not the way it works.

God wants you to be properly motivated. Look at what God did for us through Jesus Christ (cf. John 3:16). Giving and loving are intrinsically tied.

This is how God showed his love among us:
He sent his one and only Son into the world
that we might live through him. (I John 4:9)

Because God loved, He gave. That should be our motivation as well. If you love, you'll give. But not only that, you should love and give because God loved and gave. We have an example in His Son, Jesus Christ. He left heaven, came down to earth, humbled himself, and "became obedient onto death, even to the death on the cross" (cf. Philippians 2:8). He did that for you and me. He gave. And if you and I can be motivated by the fact that we want to be more Christ-like, we will give because Christ gave.

Giving Like Christ, Becoming Like Christ

As you and I give as Christ gave, we become more like Him. 2 Corinthians 3:18 reminds us:

And we, who with unveiled faces all reflect the Lord's glory, are being transformed into his likeness with ever-increasing glory, which comes from the Lord, who is the Spirit.

That's the glorious process of sanctification. You and I are supposed to be made over and over into holiness from glory to glory to glory. You and I should be more Christlike in our walk, in our talk, in our activity and in our interaction. One of the ways we can do that is tapping into the heart of God. That means loving like God loves. If we do that, then we'll automatically give. No greater love than to sacrifice, no greater love than to give (cf. John 15:13). That is and must be our motivation.

As Paul continued to explain to the Corinthians:

10 And here is my advice about what is best for you in this matter: Last year you were

the first not only to give but also to have the desire to do so. 11 Now finish the work, so that your eager willingness to do it may be matched by your completion of it, according to your means. 12 For if the willingness is there, the gift is acceptable according to what one has, not according to what he does not have. 13 Our desire is not that others might be relieved while you are hard pressed, but that there might be equality.

Paul was saying, "Good job. I see you. You filled out the commitment card. You dropped it in the offering basket. Now finish the work, so that your follow-through will match your apparent desire." Come on, how many things do we start enthusiastically and commit to and then not follow through? You start out all excited and go to your pastor and tell him what God has laid on your heart to do. And then you are empowered and set up to do it. And then it just kind of fizzles away. That's what the apostle Paul is warning against here. Don't just start strong; finish well (cf. 2 Timothy 4:7).

What Is the Right Measure of Giving?

Verses 12-13 also reveal *the measure of giving*. There is a measure associated with giving (v.12), and the measure is in proportion to what you have. Paul says give according to your means. Give according to what you have, not according to what you don't have. That way, there will be equality (v.13). If everybody gives according to what they have, then you don't have to be concerned that the absolute amount is lower or higher than what someone else gave. All *you* have to do is give according to what you have, not according to what you don't have.

If you do not have a $500,000 a year job, you do not have to worry about giving the kind of resources that somebody with that job contributes. If you are a student with a part-time job at Starbucks working 20 hours per week and you make $10,000 a year, simply give *according to* those resources. We do not need to ever get hung up on who's giving the most money.

As a little boy, I recall that my grandmother's church used to publish everyone's offering contribution in the weekly Sunday bulletin. I would scan the amounts searching for the largest numbers and then find out who gave the money. I never paid any attention to the small numbers. I was only impressed with the big ones. I suspect I was not the only one who did this! You should be grateful that God does not look at giving the way I did.

Jesus remarked in Luke 21:2-3 that the widow who gave two small coins actually gave more than the rich who were putting in their offering because she gave out of her poverty. It wasn't about the absolute amount, it was about the proportion. She put in all she had to live on.

What Is the Right Method of Giving?

Let's pause and "double-click" on I Corinthians 16:2 so we can see not only the measure of giving but also *the method of giving*. God is not just going to tell us what to do, He is even going to lay out how we should do it:

On the first day of every week, each one of you
should set aside a sum of money in keeping

with his income, saving it up, so that when I come no collections will have to be made.

This one little verse shows us the method. The method of giving is this: *giving should first and foremost be prioritized.* That is why it is done on the first day of the week. Not on the last day, not with the leftovers, not after you've paid all your bills, gotten your hair and nails done, and bought your tickets to your favorite sporting event or concert. If that is your habit, I guarantee you that God is not going to be honored because He is going to receive only the leftovers from you. If consumption dominates your money allocation recipe, and you don't put God in *first*, there will be little left.

Not only should your giving be *prioritized*, it should be *patterned*. There should be a systematic way that you give. You and I should be giving every single week. If you bring it every single week, then you will get into the habit of giving for a living. Then it's not based on some special appeal for a particular ministry at the church like a food/clothing giveaway or similar outreach program. It's not based upon whether you hear a great message from the pulpit to which you want to respond. It won't matter whether or not it's Christmas time, the "season of giving." No, you will understand that it's always time to give. Give every week, the first day of every week, and it will be prioritized and patterned.

Paul goes on to tell the Corinthians that every one of them should give. It should be *personal*. He says every one of you should take up this as your personal charge and responsibility. Don't hide amongst the group. This applies to you as an individual.

And then, Paul says we should set aside a sum of money. That means that your giving should *be planned.* You plan other things in your life, don't you? You plan to go on vacation, you plan your entertainment, you plan to catch the necessary train you in order to get to work on time. We seem to be great planners when it's something that we want to do. You should also be planning to give. You should never be caught off guard or surprised by your personal responsibility to give on a recurring basis. You simply plan for it and do it. Every week. All year round. It's just what you do. It's giving for a living.

Lastly, Paul tells the Corinthians that each is to give as God has prospered him. Your giving should *be proportional*. If your giving is proportional then no matter what you make or you don't make, all you need concern yourself with is giving in proportion to what you have, not in proportion to what you don't have.

The Magnificence of Giving

Now that we have "double-clicked" on I Corinthians 16:2, let's return to our main text in 2 Corinthians 8. Verses 14-15 say:

> **14 At the present time your plenty will supply what they need, so that in turn their plenty will supply what you need. Then there will be equality, 15 as it is written: "He who gathered much did not have too much, and he who gathered little did not have too little."**

These verses reveal the *magnificence of giving*. The quote in verse 15 is a reference to the children of Israel gathering manna in the wilderness (Exodus 16:17-18). When the manna fell, some of the Israelites gathered much and some little. Some people were, of course, older and were probably not able to get as much, and some people who were younger and stronger and no doubt more vigilant in terms of the gathering. However regardless of who collected what amount, there was equality in the distribution. If someone had much, he shaved off some and gave it to someone who had little. At the end of the day, everybody's needs were met.

So Paul reminded the Corinthians that Macedonia got in on the giving before, and now they too needed to get in the giving, knowing that as they had need later, members of the body of Christ would come to their aid. And God is standing behind the body of Christ with the ability to supply all of the needs. If you don't believe that, you won't get in on what God is doing.

When I first began to date my wife back in high school, I asked her if I could have a piece of her candy. She had two. She replied, "If I give you one, I'll only have one left." That really bothered me at the time. She had two! Now praise God that was a loooong time ago and she no longer has that mind-set (my sweetie would give me all her candy now).

That's how many of us act with God. We tell him, "No, if I give you this money than I will only have this much left." I understand that's what you have left, but you don't understand what can happen in the economy of God in terms of you being able to honor Him with your money. You can receive something that you don't see in front of you. That is the magnificence of giving. Equality is sought such that when you're lacking you can be supplied by others in the body of Christ and when you have plenty you can supply others in the body of Christ.

The Mystery of Grace

There's a mystery here, that mystery is *grace*. Let's return to 2 Corinthians 8 and look at the *mystery of giving*. Notice how

83

many times the word *grace* appears in the passage. It's mentioned four times (verses 1, 6, 7 and 9). There is one more reference to grace that I'll mention that is found 2 Corinthians 9:

> **And God is able to make all *grace* abound to you, so that in all things at all times, having all that you need, you will abound in every good work (v. 8, *emphasis mine*)**

Grace! Giving is about grace. There is a grace exchange, beloved, that you get in on when you give. *It's not about money, it's about grace.* Paul begins 2 Corinthians 8 describing the grace that God *had given* to the Macedonian churches. God gave them grace to see that they needed to give. He then gave grace so that they could have the mind-set to follow through and do it. Then he encourages the Corinthians, just like he did the Macedonians, to get in on this act of grace.

To summarize: You have received grace so you can give grace, and when you give grace because you received grace, you can expect to get grace back. But you don't just get back the grace you gave, God is able to make *all* grace abound to you. So you get more than you give!

That's difficult for you and me to understand, but that's the mystery of giving in God's economy. He says if you understand the grace that you receive, it will make you act in grace. Then when you act in grace, you will get grace back. And when you get grace back, you get surpassing grace. He says "I'll give you all that you need so that at *all* times, having *all* that you need, you will abound in every good work." He says if you get in on this grace exchange, you'll never stop giving. It's not about the money. *It's all about the grace.*

Don't you need grace? Lord, I need your grace, your unmerited favor, that's what I crave, that's what I need. I can't make it in this life without it. If not for God's grace, we would not even be saved, bound for heaven (cf. Ephesians 2:8–9). And so grace is what started us here. If not for God's grace, we could not stand (cf. Romans 5:2). Because you have grace, you need to give grace.

Now I hope you realize that you are not the only one that gives in proportion to what you have. You remember that Philippians 4:19 says:

19 And my God will meet all your needs *according to* his glorious riches in Christ Jesus. (*emphasis mine*)

"According to" once again indicates proportion. But according to what? His riches in glory. God gives to you according to what He has and what he has is *infinite*. And when you serve a God who has everything, owns everything, controls everything and sustains everything, you can trust that He can make everything happen for you that He desires. So He gives and He can make all grace abound towards you so that in all times, all of your needs will be met (all, all, all!). He is not telling you to do anything that He is not doing for you. You give according to what you have and He'll give according to what He has. You want to get in on that or not? I know I do. That's the mystery of giving.

Before we even begin to talk about the specifics of giving in terms of tithing, I want to encourage you to accept the foundational truths we have discussed. Have the right mind-set. Understand the mandate, motivation, measure, method, magnificence, and—most importantly—the mystery of giving. If you and I can grasp this, it will revolutionize how we think of the stewardship of our lives, such that we will gravitate toward a place where we will be giving for a living, not giving for a getting.

Here is a prayer for such grace: *Father, in the name of Jesus, we pray that you will bless us as you did the Macedonian church. Give us the grace of the knowledge of how you gave to us. Help us to know that giving is about sacrifice, selflessness, sharing and submitting, Father. We know that by your grace you gave, by your grace you humbled yourself in the person of Jesus Christ, by your grace you were an example to us before we ever did anything. You sacrificed for us your very life that we might even enjoy the salvation that we have. And, Father, You want us to continue to get in on this grace exchange. You desire that we give out of the proportion of what we have, knowing that you will supply us out of the proportion that you have.*

Father, help us to develop the mind-set of giving. I pray that not one of us will fail to make a commitment to begin to honor you with our financial resources. Help us to all be good stewards. Help us to look ahead, then plan ahead and then finally move ahead.

In Jesus' precious name we do pray, Amen.

Discussion Questions

1. What are the attitudes of the right mindset for giving, as the author lists at the beginning of the chapter? Do you have a right mindset?
2. Oftentimes, there is a wrong motivation for giving. Does this hinder you from giving? Or does it make

you give for the wrong reasons? Does seeing the wrong motivation in others stop you from giving?

3. Think about the method of giving, mentioned in 1 Corinthians 16:2. What are the steps to the method of giving? How can you incorporate these into your life?

4. Think about how the grace of God is tied into the concept of giving. How should this change your attitude towards giving?

CHAPTER 5:
THE GREATNESS OF GIVING

How to Allocate Your Money

0%, is our allocation to debt in order to stop greed.

10% goes to giving because we need to sow to God.

20% is targeted for savings/investing so that we might save for goals.

30% is set aside for taxes, so we can support the government.

40% is left for consumption so that we can satisfy with goods.

Near the end of King David's life, the Lord let the king know he could not begin to build the temple. Instead his son Solomon would do it all (2 Samuel 7:12-13). Nevertheless, David collected a bounty of resources to be used for that work, and he also encouraged the people to contribute to the effort (1 Chronicles 29:2-9) Look at David's words of praise to God and commitment to the work:

> **10 David praised the LORD in the presence of the whole assembly, saying,**
>
> **"Praise be to you, O LORD, God of our father Israel, from everlasting to everlasting. 11 Yours, O LORD, is the greatness and the power and the glory and the majesty and the splendor, for everything in heaven and earth is yours. Yours, O LORD, is the kingdom; you are exalted as head over all. 12 Wealth**

**and honor come from you; you are the ruler
of all things. In your hands are strength and
power to exalt and give strength to all. 13
Now, our God, we give you thanks, and praise
your glorious name. (I Chronicles 29:10-13)**

Take the next several days and when you wake up in the
morning, proclaim this passage of Scripture out loud. If you
do, it should affect the way you go through the rest of the day.
The affirmation, that everything—the greatness, power, glory,
majesty, splendor, *everything* in heaven and earth—is God's
should affect our daily walk in such a way that we understand
we don't own anything.

Moses on God's Goodness

A similar reminder appears in Deuteronomy 8:15–18.
Moses is speaking to the children of Israel in anticipation of
their entering the land of promise, noting how God led them
through the wilderness that included serpents, scorpions, and
drought, and that He fed them manna. He calls on the people to
**remember the LORD your God, for it is he who gives you
the ability to produce wealth, and so confirms his covenant,
which he swore to your forefathers, as it is today. (v.18)**

It is one thing to trust God while you're waiting for something, but it's another thing entirely to trust Him once you
receive it. Many of us spend much time praying for something we want, whether it's a new job, new opportunity, or new
resources. Once our prayers are answered, we forget about God.
Moses knew the children of Israel might do the same, so he
spends time reminding them about what God has done. Spend
the next several days meditating on this Scripture passage as

well. It will help you to remember that everything is in His hands. He is the provider of everything, and He is the one who gives us the ability to produce what we have.

Honoring the God of All the Earth

And so with that backdrop, let us be reminded that we are stewards and not owners. That cannot be emphasized enough. What you and I do next shows what we really believe about God. Is He truly the God of all the earth? Then we need to honor and praise Him with every bit of our lives, not just with our voices, not just with our time, not just with our talent but also with our treasure. It should all line up if we are going to have an understanding of the greatness of giving.

At the very beginning of this chapter I highlighted the second parameter in the money recipe which is a 10 percent allocation to giving in order to sow to God.

The previous chapter laid the foundation for giving, and as we discussed proportional giving (2 Corinthians 8:11–12). The proportional giving example that we see in Scripture and hear spoken of from most pulpits is *tithing*. The word *tithe* actually means a tenth. Tithing is the guide that we have and the biblical principle that we apply today. Many people think that tithing is tied to the Old Testament law and should no longer be in operation. Actually, if you look in your Bible, over four hundred years before the law was even given Abram (God would later change his name to Abraham) practiced tithing (see Genesis 14:17-20). Also in Genesis 28:20-22, we see Abraham's grandson Jacob do something similar. It would appear that there was a custom in the society in which these patriarchs lived that if you wanted to honor and reverence somebody then you not only did it with your words, but you did it with your possessions. The acceptable amount that would accomplish that goal was a gift of a tenth.

We can safely conclude that tithing honors the one to whom it is given. It is a show of respect and it is a show of reverence. Proverbs 3:9 reminds us to

Honor the LORD with your wealth, with the firstfruits of all your crops;

The Scripture explains that you honor the Lord with your material goods: As Moses wrote,

22 Be sure to set aside a tenth of all that your fields produce each year. 23 Eat the tithe of your grain, new wine and oil, and the first-born of your herds and flocks in the presence of the LORD your God at the place he will choose as a dwelling for his Name, so that you may learn to revere the LORD your God always. (Deuteronomy 14:22-23)

Giving is about Reverence, Worship

Why did God ask His people to tithe? You and I both know that God does not need any resources. Everything there is He created, and He sustains. It is all for Him, to Him, by Him, and through Him, and He possesses it all. Verse 23 tells us that He is looking for His people to fear, or reverence Him, *always*. We value those things on which we spend our money. As a matter of fact, we can sometimes *worship* those things on which we spend our money (think about it). This is about reverence. This is about respect. This is about worship. This is *not* about the money in your pocket and God trying to separate you from it (or me trying to separate you from it). God says if you honor me with your resources, you will be learning to fear me, always. That's what He desires.

So the children of Israel were commanded to honor God by tithing. What's interesting is it appears that there were two, possibly three tithes that the Lord asked of His people. No, I am not suggesting that you give 30 percent of your money. I am simply reminding us of some of the parameters concerning this subject.

The first tithe for the nation was given to provide for the priestly order of Levi ((Numbers 18:20–21). Since the Levites did not receive land as an inheritance (God was their inheritance) like the other tribes, they were to sustain themselves on the tithe collected while they dedicated themselves to serving before the Lord. This was the first tithe.

The second tithe, or what I would call the festival tithe, is referred to in Deuteronomy 14: 22-26, and is an annual tithe of one's crops and livestock.

Then every third year, the people participated in another tithe, described in Deuteronomy 26. (Some scholars would argue that that this third-year tithe would replace the festival tithe, so that is why I said there were at least two, if not three). Just like with today, that tithe is not a forced thing. It is a matter of conscience.

12 When you have finished setting aside a tenth of all your produce in the third year, the year of the tithe, you shall give it to the Levite, the alien, the fatherless and the widow, so that they may eat in your towns

and be satisfied. 13 Then say to the LORD your God: "I have removed from my house the sacred portion and have given it to the Levite, the alien, the fatherless and the widow, according to all you commanded. I have not turned aside from your commands nor have I forgotten any of them. 14 I have not eaten any of the sacred portion while I was in mourning, nor have I removed any of it while I was unclean, nor have I offered any of it to the dead. I have obeyed the LORD my God; I have done everything you commanded me. 15 Look down from heaven, your holy dwelling place, and bless your people Israel and the land you have given us as you promised on oath to our forefathers, a land flowing with milk and honey."
(Deuteronomy 26:12-15)

Look at the progression. You should be able to say "God, I have done what you've commanded me to do. Now, I desire that you bless us and the land you have given us." *The blessing is based upon obedience.* If you can voice this "vow of compliance," you can pray, "Bless me, Lord, please bless me."

Bless me based on what? Bless me based on the fact that my life lines up with what you require. That's an easy prayer for God to answer. I believe it becomes a much more difficult prayer for God to answer if you and I live ragged lives that do not honor Him.

You and I should be able to say, "I have honored you, God. I am not faultless and I am not sinless, but I am blameless before you because the things that I have done wrong I have made right through confession of my sin" (see 1 John 1:9). That's a whole different prayer. It is a respectful prayer of anticipation and expectation. It's based on the fact that you have made an effort to honor God, and one of the ways that you have done what is right concerns your handling of the sacred portion (v. 13).

The Choice: To Honor . . .Or Rob . . God

You may say, "Well, I'm not honoring God with my resources, so I can't voice this vow of compliance. Oh well . . ." It's not like the options are honor God or don't honor God. It's either honor God or rob Him. This brings us to one of the best-known passages of Scripture on tithing in Malachi 3:8–10. (Now you could not have grown up in the African-American church tradition and not have heard someone with a booming voice read this passage during the offering time).

To understand the Malachi passage fully, let's begin with verse 6:

> **6 "I the LORD do not change. So you, O descendants of Jacob, are not destroyed. 7 Ever since the time of your forefathers you have turned away from my decrees and have not kept them. Return to me, and I will return to you," says the LORD Almighty. "But you ask, `How are we to return?' 8"Will a man rob God? Yet you rob me. "But you ask, `How do we rob you?'**

"In tithes and offerings. 9 You are under a curse—the whole nation of you—because you are robbing me. 10 Bring the whole tithe into the storehouse, that there may be food in my house. Test me in this," says the LORD Almighty, "and see if I will not throw open the floodgates of heaven and pour out so much blessing that you will not have room enough for it.

Everybody else is shifting and constantly changing, but God is right here and He does not change (see Hebrews 13:8). And because He does not change, He promised His people that He would not consume them. They will always be His chosen people.

God goes on to tell His people that they are not honoring Him with their resources, and if they are not honoring Him, then they are actually robbing Him. Now what are you robbing God of if you do not honor Him with your resources? You are not robbing him of resources; you are robbing Him of *glory*. Glory is what is due Him. He deserves all the glory, all the honor, all the praise, our very lives. If we do not give Him that then we're robbing Him.

That is why it's so dangerous not to have everything in your life lined up with what God requires, including your checkbook. If we do not live in such a way that God is honored, we actually rob Him. Think about Romans 3:23 within the context of this discussion. That familiar verse simply says,

for all have sinned and fall short of the glory of God,

Disobedience cannot bring God glory and when we sin, we cannot fulfill the purpose for which we are designed. What purpose is that? Like all creatures, we were created to give God glory! The true devastation of sin is that it keeps us from doing our job.

So how do we fix this robbing of God (v. 9)? Verse 10 tells us we need to bring our tithe to God. If we do what God requires, He promises us an abundant blessing. He basically declares that we cannot out-give Him. The sacrifice you give pales in comparison to what God can pour into your life, and what He has already poured into your life. Remember, **"God so loved the world He gave His only begotten son"** (John 3:16 KJV). So, even if He never gave us anything else, those of us who have received Jesus Christ as personal savior have already been given eternal life. He gave us life because He loved us. Now we should give because we love Him.

However, God says, "Test me . . .and see if I will not throw open the floodgates of heaven" for you. If you follow the premise, then you can claim the promise. As we have previously discussed, Philippians 4:19 says something very similar when it says:

And my God will meet all your needs according to his glorious riches in Christ Jesus

He can bless in proportion to what He has. What does He have? His riches in glory. Malachi 3:10 tells us God can throw open the windows of heaven and pour out a truly abundant blessing. Out of what supply? His riches in glory.

Your entire life must honor God. *The key to your life is
obedience.* Obedience will include every area of your life,
including your finances.

I do not want to be a glory robber. Please realize that you
rob God in other ways besides your finances. Again, giving is
not the deodorant for a stinky life. *Giving is a demonstration of
obedience.* Your entire life must honor God. I don't want you
to think that the key to your life is giving. No, *the key to your
life is obedience.* If you listen to some TV preachers, they will
give you the impression that if you just start giving, everything
in your life will turn around. "Sow a seed, and it will come
back to you." No, it is about a demonstration of your love
for Christ through sacrifice. That is obedience, and obedience
by definition will include every area of your life, including
your finances.

I'll say it again: *the key to your life is obedience.* Therefore,
honor Him and do not rob Him of His glory.

Three Ways Our Tithe Honors God

The tithe is the biblical example of honoring God with
your finances. When you tithe, you are supporting three very
important things. The first is that *you are supporting God's
plans.* When you give to your local church, you're supporting
God's plans.

God has given every local church body a vision, mission and plans for what He wants them to do to advance the
kingdom of God. When you give your tithes to your local

church fellowship, you are supporting God's plans as outlined in the church's vision and mission. You help that church bring kingdom light to the community it serves.

Second, when you tithe *you are supporting God's pastors.* As Paul wrote:

> **Anyone who receives instruction in the word must share all good things with his instructor. (Galatians 6:6)**

If you've been taught the Word, you need to give back to those who teach the Word. Pastors need to be supported, similarly to the way that the Levites were supported in the Old Testament. The Levites had no inheritance, so the children of Israel were instructed to support them while they handled God's tabernacle work (Numbers 18:20–21). Now, God's body, the church, should support those who do His work. Again, the apostle Paul instructed:

> **17 The elders who direct the affairs of the church well are worthy of double honor, especially those whose work is preaching and teaching. 18 For the Scripture says, "Do not muzzle the ox while it is treading out the grain," and "The worker deserves his wages." (1 Timothy 5:17–18).**

To the believers in Corinth, the apostle added this admonition:

> **13 Don't you know that those who work in the temple get their food from the temple, and**

**those who serve at the altar share in what is
offered on the altar? 14 In the same way, the
Lord has commanded that those who preach
the gospel should receive their living from
the gospel. (1 Corinthians 9:13-14)**

These verses help us to see that when we support the church
through giving tithes, we not only support God's plans, we also
rightly support God's pastors.

Third, when you tithe *you are supporting God's place*. It is
important to keep the physical structure of the church building
in good working order. Repairs, maintenance and improve-
ments need to be made on an ongoing basis so that the building
can serve the people of God and the community at large. In 2
Kings 12:4-5, 11–12, King Joash bemoaned the temple's state
of disrepair. He commanded that offerings be given and that
craftsmen be assigned to restore the temple to its previous glory:

**4 Joash said to the priests, "Collect all the
money that is brought as sacred offerings
to the temple of the LORD—the money collected in the census, the money received from
personal vows and the money brought volun-
tarily to the temple. 5 Let every priest receive
the money from one of the treasurers, and
let it be used to repair whatever damage is
found in the temple." 11 When the amount
had been determined, they gave the money
to the men appointed to supervise the work
on the temple. With it they paid those who
worked on the temple of the LORD—the
carpenters and builders, 12 the masons and**

**stonecutters. They purchased timber and
dressed stone for the repair of the temple of
the LORD, and met all the other expenses of
restoring the temple.**

King Joash made it a priority to use a portion of the
resources collected to take care of the temple building. For
those of us who worship in church structures, we must do the
same. We should do it not so that our buildings can be pristine
monuments, but so they can be functional instruments that can
bring God glory.

Why We Give

Fundamentally, the greatness of giving is revealed in three
ways. Number one, *giving shows gratitude for the past.* We
base our giving upon all that God has done; we give to show
our thankfulness and gratitude for His expression of care in our
lives. That's why King David began his prayer in 1 Chronicles
29 with praise to the Lord. He extolled God's virtues (vs. 10–11)
and remembered His goodness and favor toward the children
of Israel (vs. 11–12). That shows an understanding of who God
is and what God has done. So when we give, we are acknowledging that God is God and we're demonstrating gratitude for
what He has done in the past.

Showing gratitude for the past brings *clarity.* To see a clear
path for the future, remember who has blessed you and how
much He has blessed you. That's why I suggest starting the
next several days with the confession of 1 Chronicles 29:10–13.
The world would tell you that is not clarity, that's absurdity.
"Giving your hard-earned money to someone you've never seen
or met makes no sense. You've got to make your own way in

life because there really is no God." Oh, but He is real. I've seen His works; I've seen His majesty. I've seen what He's done. Therefore, I have no other recourse but to praise Him, to thank Him, give Him gratitude, and give and support His plans and His pastor's and His place. Showing God gratitude is not absurdity, it is clarity.

Second, *giving allows grounding in the present.* How so? When you give, it is a constant reminder that your life is not all about you. What a marvelous perspective and what a marvelous reward that God allows! Each time you sit down and you write a check for God's work, you are acknowledging on a consistent basis that life is bigger than you. You are reminded that there are things going on in the body of Christ, and you are just a part of what God is doing Every time you are allowed the opportunity to give, it should humble you. You realize afresh that there is not only a contributor of the gift, but there is a consumer of the gift, and, more importantly, there is also a creator of the gift. If you never give, you do not get that reminder. Your world can become increasingly small and you can lose the perspective that everything is *not* about you.

I would say that allowing grounding in the present brings an *opportunity.* The world would say it brings a liability. The world would say that it's a liability to recognize other people and other people's contributions. The world would tell you that it is indeed all about you. To think that it is not about you may do damage to your self-esteem and sense of self-worth. "You must retain control over your life and acknowledging others may erode that control." But God would tell you, and I would tell you that it is not a liability to give, that it is indeed an opportunity—an opportunity for you to be reminded that it's not all about you!

Third, *giving provides growth for the future.* You and I have an opportunity to lay up treasure in heaven (Luke 16:9; Matthew 6:19–21). According to 2 Corinthians 9:10, we can enlarge our harvest of our righteousness. Also, the better we execute our job as stewards, the more our master will trust us with in the future (Luke 19:17, 19).

Now I would conclude that providing growth for the future brings *security.* The world would say it brings calamity. Society would tell you that you are out of your mind to give resources away with talk of laying up treasure in heaven. You could be using those resources now to build yourself bigger barns (like the rich fool in Luke 12:18.) If you do not, nonbelievers would tell you. "You're out of your mind, because you're going to need that stuff later. Give your money away now and you are inviting calamity." I say it is security to trade what you cannot keep to gain what you cannot lose.

Old vs. New

Now you might say to yourself, "Well, tithing is not commanded in the New Testament. It's an Old Testament thing." You are correct, it is not commanded in the New Testament, but it is *commended* in the New Testament. In Matthew 23:23 Jesus says to the Pharisees:

> **"Woe to you, teachers of the law and Pharisees, you hypocrites! You give a tenth of your spices—mint, dill and cummin. But you have neglected the more important matters of the law—justice, mercy and faithfulness. You should have practiced the latter, without neglecting the former.**

God wants and deserves everything from you because He gave you everything.

The Pharisees were so observant that they were even tithing the spices that they kept in their homes. However, Jesus told them that they were neglecting the more important matters of the law. They should have practiced the latter (meaning justice, mercy, and faithfulness) without neglecting the former, which is tithing. So Jesus commended tithing. That's why I can say again, it's not about the money. It's about *everything*. God wants everything. Why? Because He paid for you and He owns you (1 Corinthians 6:19–20). Jesus did not command that we tithe, but He commended we do so without neglecting the weightier matters of the law. Tithing is a guide, and it's a good one.

Start with a Plan to Give

In 1993 my wife, Kim, and I bought our first house in South Holland, a suburb of Chicago. We bought that house on two incomes, both working outside the home. At that time we vowed that we would not go into a situation where we made a major purchase, such as a house, but had not yet honored God with our giving. Early in our marriage, we understood the importance of tithing, but based upon our past decisions (reflected in our present obligations) we literally could not begin at once to give 10 percent of our money. You may be in the same place where you don't have much of anything left after all the bills are paid. Let me encourage you to start somewhere. You have to have a plan.

When Kim and I decided we wanted to honor God with our money, we worked our way up. I don't remember where we started (maybe 3 percent or 4 percent), but we were determined to realign everything we did so that we could get to 10 percent of our incomes. I can't recall exactly how long it took us (perhaps eighteen months to two years), but we steadily increased until we were able to tithe properly. We cut expenses and gave the savings. When we received raises, we did not consume the additional money; we gave it back to God. We were purposeful about honoring God with our money, so by the time we purchased our house we were tithing.

Beware the Temptation to Cut the Tithe

In 1995, Kim and I were expecting our second child (a wonderful little girl who we would name Courtney). Kim's granny was the person who provided daycare for our firstborn, Kendall, at the time and we anticipated she would care for both of our children after the birth. However, Granny fell ill and she passed away about a month before Courtney was born. So the person that we thought was going to be able to take care of both of our children was not with us. That meant that we needed to put daycare expenses into a budget that I would describe as already tight. Kim did not really want to consider non-family daycare and felt strongly this was the time to begin her season of staying home and being with the kids. Well, we did what anybody else in the world does—we looked at the numbers. What do the numbers tell us about the mortgage payment? What do the numbers tell us about that reality that we bought the house on *two* incomes?

The numbers weighed in with a conclusion—*it cannot be done*. So now it is time to see what can be cut. At the time, Kim was in the first year of pursuing her MBA at Northwestern, with her company picking up 80 percent of the tab. Business school was the first thing to go, because we lost her company's assistance when she left, and we could not afford to pay 100 percent of the *cost*. (Praise Note: Eleven years later, Kim graduated with her MBA from Northwestern in 2006). We continued to cut and chop and tallied up all that was coming in and all that was going out. We took away Kim's income and then looked at the bottom line. There was a deficit of about $1,100 a month!

The voice of the world played in my head and said, *Review your budget again. I see something that you could cut that would save you several hundred dollars a month. Your tithe. You're trying to make it work, right? Get rid of the tithe. You can cut that deficit way down. You'd be irresponsible if you didn't. Surely God would understand.*

I remember Kim and me saying to ourselves that we were not touching God's money no matter what. We were committed to continue to give and trust that God would provide a way for us to get through this financial crunch. If Kim being home during this season to focus on the children was what God wanted us to do (and through prayer and petition we felt it was), we believed that God always provides where He guides, and He always protects where He directs. But until you get to a place where you are staring down a deficit of $1,100 a month or something to that effect, you might not ever test your belief that God is able. So we began to look at it a little differently.

How did we deal with that temptation to reduce or even eliminate our tithe to the Lord? We believed that God was calling us to have Kim stay home *and* not touch His money either! We put pen to paper and began to determine how we could make this thing work.

Eventually we found a way. We cashed in Kim's 401k retirement money. You may ask, "Why take a long-term investment and then cash it in?" Our answer: We took an investment from one place and we invested it in another place—our family. The return was not on a monthly financial statement. The return was seen in our children. We took money that the world would tell us we were crazy to touch and invested it, not in some get-rich-quick scheme, but in kingdom and family building.

A few weeks after our second child was born, Kim went back to work for about two months; then she gave her notice. It was June, 1995. Now we are face to face with this $1,100 deficit that we plan to address with this 401k pension money. Yet as we looked out over the time horizon, we knew this was a temporary fix. The money eventually would run out. We came to a crossroads: Would we trust God or trust our well-developed worldly instincts? We decided to trust God. And guess what God did? In August of 1995 I got a new job making more money. Within a year, we replaced Kim's former income with my salary increase! We no longer were concerned about the mortgage and we did not have the $1,100 monthly deficit that we had at the outset. We did what God required, we did not dishonor Him by touching His money, and we stayed faithful.

As we did His will, He blessed us, and He met all our needs. About a year after that I accepted an opportunity to become a partner at a private equity firm in Connecticut. The increase that we have seen in our lives in terms of our finances has been exponential since we made the decision not to dishonor God but to trust Him. I am not telling you things that I haven't lived. This is not theoretical or hypothetical for me. I am telling you that God is able to make all grace abound towards you, even when you're staring at a monthly deficit of $1,100. *God is able!*

Depending on when you are reading this, you may be shortly receiving an IRS tax refund. *Oh no, preacher don't mess with my refund check.* Sorry. What better way if you are not tithing now (that is, giving 10 percent of your *gross* household income) to move closer to that commitment than to not consume that anticipated refund as you had planned? You must look ahead, plan ahead and move ahead. Contributing your refund check would move you from whatever level of giving you are currently, closer to the 10 percent of gross income that the tithe represents.

You might be saying, "I had plans for that money! We were going to get new furniture, go on vacation, or splurge on a shopping spree." Look, I am just a preacher but if you are serious about change you will honor God by doing something different with those resources.

You know what God is requiring. Move deliberately toward honoring God with 10 percent of your earnings. This is the proportion that the Bible reflects and commends. If you are sincere, you will find ways to reprioritize your finances to do so.

You must start somewhere, and the sooner the better. You will be surprised what you can do as you yield yourself to God as a vessel fit for His use. Stop asking yourself how you can afford to tithe, and start asking yourself how you can afford not to!

Discussion Questions:

1. In what way is the body of Christ supposed to support the elders of the church? Find the Scriptures related to this question and expound on what God has called the body of Christ to do for the elders of the church.

2. Think about the three ways our giving honors God. In which of these ways (or all three of them) has God directed you in your giving?

3. In Matthew 23:23 Jesus says to the Pharisees, "Woe to you, teachers of the law and Pharisees, you hypocrites! Why did Jesus rebuke them this way?

4. If you were faced with a financial crisis situation what would be your first reaction in handling the problem? How would you show God that you trust Him to help you through the situation?

CHAPTER 6:
THE BIBLICAL WISDOM OF SAVING AND INVESTING

How to Allocate Your Money

0% is our allocation to debt in order to stop greed.

10% goes to giving because we need to sow to God.

20% is targeted for savings/investing so that we might save for goals.

30% is set aside for taxes, so we can support the government.

40% is left for consumption so that we can satisfy with goods.

If we want to manage our finances the way God would have us manage them, we need to know what the Bible says about saving and investing. Let's turn to Proverbs 6:6–11 to partake of the wisdom of Solomon.

6 Go to the ant, you sluggard; consider its ways and be wise!

7 It has no commander, no overseer or ruler,

8 yet it stores its provisions in summer and gathers its food at harvest.

9 How long will you lie there, you sluggard? When will you get up from your sleep?

10 A little sleep, a little slumber, a little folding of the hands to rest—

11 and poverty will come on you like a bandit and scarcity like an armed man.

What's with the name-calling, Solomon? Seems to me Solomon pens these words with a certain sense of frustration. It's as though he is saying, "If you would just observe the simplest things, you could learn something, but you don't learn because you don't look. So, go to the ant, and see what it is doing. It has no alarm clock to wake it up. The sense of responsibility wakes the ant up in the morning for it to do what it needs to do. Nobody has to hold its hand and tell it everything it needs to do—like you. The ant is a *saver*. The ant is a *worker*. The ant is *one who sows and then reaps*."

In verse 9, it is almost as if Solomon is talking to someone who is not convinced about the truth of his words. I can imagine his question, "How long will you lie there, you lazy bum?" being posed to somebody who is sitting on the coach with the football game on and a huge bowl of pretzels, cheese puffs, and potato chips with crumbs everywhere. Solomon is looking at him and saying, "How long are you going to lie there and just eat pretzels, cheese puffs and potato chips while there is work that needs to be done?!" So he adds an additional admonition in verses 10–11 about sleeping the day away and it consequences. Let me paraphrase those verses for you:

"If you don't wake up and start working for the future, you will wind up with little or nothing. It will feel like you have been robbed at gunpoint by two guys named Poverty and Scarcity, who snuck up behind you and took everything you had."

In his book *Your Money Counts*, Howard Dayton writes that savings is provision for tomorrow while debt is presumption on tomorrow. If you and I are going to save, then we must forego something today so that you can have something tomorrow. You must *give up consuming today.*

In our money recipe, the target for savings is 20 percent (yes, 20 percent!). The phrase to associate with savings is "save for goals." Most Americans save less than 5 percent because we consume almost everything that we get. Why? Because we are never content. Somebody once asked John D. Rockefeller, the oil magnate who helped found Standard Oil Company, "How much is enough?" His reply was, "Just a little bit more." He was a multimillionaire (back when a million dollars really meant something!) and was he satisfied? Apparently not, because he was still chasing a little bit more. However, the Bible teaches us that godliness with contentment is great gain (1 Timothy 6:6). The gain is not in getting more, the gain is in being content with what you have.

Budgeting: Know What's Coming In and Going Out

The first step to saving for the future is accepting the concept of *budgeting.* King Solomon advised the many farmers of Israel,

> **23 Be sure you know the condition of your flocks,**
>
> **give careful attention to your herds;**
>
> **24 for riches do not endure forever,**
>
> **and a crown is not secure for all generations. (Proverbs 27:23-24)**

Wise Solomon says you need to know what you own and what you owe. You need to know what's coming in and going out. If you never look at it, you will never know. You could well be losing a portion of your inheritance because it's leaking out in different areas and you have no idea.

One of the starting points in a budgeting process that is recommended by many financial planners/advisers is to write down everything that you spend. If you keep track of everything, even the smallest amounts, you will have a good, clear picture of what is happening with your money.

Look at where your money is going. You cannot have any expectation from your money if you have no inspection of your money.

You may say, "I don't know why I can't seem to save," or "I don't know why I don't have anything to invest," or "I don't know why I can't seem to tithe." Well, you never will unless you begin to look at where your money is going. You can't have any expectation from your money if you have no inspection of your money (know the condition of your flocks). If you do not take the time to evaluate, then ultimately what will transpire is "a little sleep . . . and a little folding of the hands to rest." Poverty and scarcity show up to your door next.

Many of us know exactly where our money is going, but others of us have no idea how much all the little things add up to leave us without the ability to save and invest for our future and support the kingdom of God. It's the *little* foxes that spoil the vineyards (Song of Solomon 2:15). The big foxes are easier to identify and you can capture them more easily. While you should definitely focus on the big foxes, don't forget about the little ones. If you get enough little foxes running through your growing crop of grapes, they'll do as much damage as one big one will. You need to know about the bills, about where all your money is going.

The Budget: AKA the S³ Plan

Somebody suggested to me that we not call a budget by that name. They felt "budget" is a pejorative name that is too restrictive. They suggested I call it a "spending plan." *Spending plan*, however, is too limiting. We are looking at a three-part plan. It's a *sowing* plan, a *saving* plan, and a *spending* plan. That's what a "budget" is really. Let's refer to it as our S³ plan.

A S³ plan should help you to focus on the sowing that you need to do, the saving that you need to do, and the spending that you need to do. If all you do is count what you take in and then look at what your current situation is, without looking at what you sow and what you save, then you just have a spending plan.

The S³ plan includes honoring God first, with the first fruits of all your increase (Proverbs 3:9). Only when you have a sowing plan in place should you then contemplate putting a saving plan in place. Once you allow for taxes (we will get to that later), the spending plan is what remains, and it falls like meat off the bone. If you show me your sowing and saving plan, I can tell you your spending plan. That's how it *should* work. That's not how it works in America, because we consume absolutely everything we possibly can, and then we consume even more because we use debt. But we need a S³ plan in place.

Three Principles of Savings:

1. Begin by Discerning Your Obligations

If you are going to save, you must apply the following three principles. The first principle is this: *If you are going to save you must have discernment.* What are you trying to discern? You must be aware of what your obligations are in order for you to save. Now savings really has a threefold focus because you have three main obligations: to provide for the former generation (your parents and grandparents), the current generation (that's you), and the future generation (your children).

I Timothy 5:8 says:

> **If anyone does not provide for his relatives, and especially for his immediate family, he has denied the faith and is worse than an unbeliever.**

This Scripture reminds us that we need to be able to take care of those in our family. That verse is part of a larger discussion the apostle Paul is having with Timothy about setting things in the proper order in the church. Earlier in chapter 5 Paul advised Timothy:

> **3 Give proper recognition to those widows who are really in need. 4 But if a widow has children or grandchildren, these should learn first of all to put their religion into practice by caring for their own family and so repaying their parents and grandparents, for this is pleasing to God.**

Paul didn't say pay the parents and grandparents; he said *repay* them. Why? *Because you owe them.* Don't you realize that you owe those who have come before you? Somebody sacrificed so that you could be here today.

My mother and my father sacrificed for me to be here. Mom was the one that was paying for those piano lessons and those saxophone lessons, those baseball uniforms and those enrichment programs. Mom was the one who was still paying the University of Pennsylvania on a monthly basis for my remaining educational bills even after I graduated. Mom was the one who did that. My Dad was the one who helped me buy my first car. Dad was the one who gave me money for an outrageous phone bill in college (mostly to my future wife, I might add) so that my credit rating would not be impacted. Dad was the one who provided a sizeable portion of the down payment on my first house and lent me money to assist with an even larger down payment on my second house. Dad was the one who did that. So if ever my parents find themselves in a place where they need assistance, they shouldn't come to the church first.

Pay back what has been paid forward. When you find out that Mama and Paw-Paw need some assistance, go to your savings and help them through their difficulties.

Paul is saying that family should recognize the debt that is owed to the previous generation and pay back what has been paid forward. If you consume everything you get, then you can't do that. If you're living check to check with no margin, you can't do that. If that's how you are living, it is probably because you have not saved the money you're supposed to save. Paul said that would actually be putting your religion (or belief) into practice and that would please God. So when you find out that Mama, Big Mama, and Paw-Paw or Madea are struggling and need some assistance, I hope you can go to your savings and help them through their difficulties. If you can't, I think that's a shame.

American culture is such an individualistic culture that a lot of people don't even see a problem with the situation that I have just described. However, in other cultures, particularly in African, Far Eastern or Middle Eastern cultures, it is a privilege to take care of those that have provided for you all these years. That's not only a privilege but a responsibility that they understand and is part of the fabric of who they are. But here in the United States, this spirit of individualism has so permeated our culture that many would respond to their elders, "You're on your own. I do not have it to give to you anyway! Please, I'm trying to get my own life together." That's not right. They sacrificed for you so that you could be where you are. Whatever job you have, whatever money you are making, if you thought you got here by yourself, you'd better recognize you didn't.

So we must lay funds aside to assist the former generation. But we also need to pay attention to the current generation. Clearly you need to provide something for yourself, your future. Things will always happen in life that are unexpected (e.g. illness with high medical bills, loss of jobs, broken relationships, fire, crime). However, we can mitigate those unexpected things that come up by setting aside resources now. Doing so will help us to better prepare for those things when they come.

Let's not forget our children, the future generation, which is our third savings focus. What is still the best way to get rich in America? <u>Inheritance</u>. A parent or relative passes on and they leave you a chunk of money.

For instance, when I was graduating from college, several of my classmates planned to take a summer trip to Europe before going to their new jobs. I couldn't *think* about doing that. I needed to start work right away. Others were able to take jobs with low salaries with commission structures (like stockbrokers). I could not think about that. My student loans told me NO. Had my family benefited from a wealth transfer from generation to generation (that had been properly managed and invested), I might have been able to consider more options. But no, I needed to start making my way right away. I owe, I owe, it's off to work I go!

Of course, an inheritance may not come soon, if your parents lives long (as you hope they will.) Or the inheritance, when it comes, may be small or even nonexistent. So you need to consider other resources for your children. That means primarily saving for their needs. 2 Corinthians 12:14 points us to the concept of passing on resources to our children as Paul writes:

> **Now I am ready to visit you for the third time, and I will not be a burden to you, because what I want is not your possessions but you. After all, children should not have to save up for their parents, but parents for their children.**

The sandwich generation consists of those among us who are beginning to take care of our parents while at the same time still sowing into our children.

Remember, Paul tells us in I Timothy 5:4 that the children should take care of the parents. Now in this passage he indicates that the parents are supposed to take care of the children. So which is it? It's not either/or, it's *both*. It can feel like a "double whammy" for those of us in the so-called "sandwich generation." The sandwich generation consists of those among us who are beginning to take care of our parents while at the same time still sowing into our children. The kids have not been to college yet and we are still trying to save for that, but our parents need us too. Many of us have it coming and going. But guess what? You must take care of all of it.

The stress that comes along with this responsibility is alleviated in part by having a savings plan that allows you to lay up resources so that when these things come, you're prepared—like the ant.

Remember the money recipe includes 20 percent to savings. Let's turn our attention to a practical biblical example of savings in Genesis 41 and we will see something very interesting. A famine would soon engulf the Middle East region, stretching from Egypt to the land of Abraham, Isaac, and Jacob. Pharaoh had two dreams about the famine, which he relayed to Jacob's son Joseph (vv. 17–24), who was in jail after being falsely accused. The Egyptian ruler could not figure the dreams' meaning, so eventually he summoned Joseph to interpret the dreams. Joseph informed him that his dreams were one and the same and that God was revealing to Pharaoh what he was about to do.

Since God was showing Pharaoh what He was about to do, the Egyptians needed to look ahead, plan ahead, and then move ahead. That is what a good steward does, and Joseph was an *excellent* steward. He had discernment from God in terms of interpreting dreams. He told Pharaoh there would seven years of great abundance, and then all the abundance in Egypt would be forgotten as a famine would ravage the land in the subsequent seven years (vs. 26–32).

Now look at Joseph's advice in verses 33–34:

> **33 "And now let Pharaoh look for a discerning and wise man and put him in charge of the land of Egypt. 34 Let Pharaoh appoint commissioners over the land to take a *fifth* of the harvest of Egypt during the seven years of abundance. (*emphasis mine*).**

When it is going well, don't consume everything you have, because the lean years are coming. Set aside something for a rainy day.

Joseph recommended that if Pharaoh wanted to survive the famine, he should set aside a fifth of the harvest. What is a fifth? Twenty percent. It would not seem like setting aside 20 percent could get you through seven years (see vv. 34–36). However, somehow the amount set aside covered the seven years so much that the Egyptians were able to meet all of their needs and then sell their abundance to the rest of the world.

There is a principle here. When it is going well, don't consume everything you have, because the lean years are coming. Set aside something for a rainy day. What is the guide? The recommendation that is right here in Scripture from Joseph is 20 percent.

Remember, the first principle you must apply if you are going to save is discernment, so you can meet the needs of the former generation (your parents), the current generation (yourself and other family members), and the next generation (your children). Fundamentally, that relates to *looking ahead* (applying it to the stewardship principles of Luke 16).

Three Principles of Savings:

2. Continue by Displaying Discipline

Here is the second savings principle: *If you are going to save you must have discipline.* You cannot do anything without discipline. The Word of God in Proverbs 21:20 helps us to understand this concept:

In the house of the wise are stores of choice food and oil, but a foolish man devours all he has.

A foolish man devours all he has—just like many of us did growing up when it came to one of our favorite candies, Now 'N Laters. I know for me, there was never any "later" with my Now 'N Laters. The package had a slogan on it: "Eat some now and save some for later." However, I do not recall anyone who said, "Oh, no, no, no. I am saving this piece for later. Maybe tomorrow, or next week sometime." It just didn't happen. They should have changed the labeling on the package to read "Now 'N Now"!

But "Now and Later" is the concept that Solomon is describing in verse 20. He says that in the wise man's house there are stores of oil and food. Notice that he did not say in the house of the rich, he said in the house of the *wise*. The stores of oil do not necessarily come because somebody has a great job or a great inheritance. You can work with what you have, honor God with your money, save, reduce your consumption, and increase your contentment. These things can all line up for you if you just work with what you have. You would be considered wise if you do not completely devour whatever it is that you have.

Proverbs 21:17 says it another way:

He who loves pleasure will become poor;
whoever loves wine and oil will never be rich.

The person who loves pleasure is one who will devour all that he has. He will respond to his appetite and choose not to store anything. That clearly is foolish behavior. You will never get where you need to get devouring all that you have, *especially* God's portion. Remember, God can do more with that 90 percent He is lending you than you can ever do with the 100 percent that you try to keep.

Look at Proverbs 24:30–34. Here Solomon is looking to emphasize the importance of discipline, but from a different angle.

30 I went past the field of the sluggard, past
the vineyard of the man who lacks judgment;

31 thorns had come up everywhere, the ground was covered with weeds, and the stone wall was in ruins. 32 I applied my heart to what I observed and learned a lesson from what I saw: 33 A little sleep, a little slumber, a little folding of the hands to rest—34 and poverty will come on you like a bandit and scarcity like an armed man.

While the sluggard was lying on the couch eating the snack foods and getting crumbs all over the couch, Solomon went out and looked at the man's field. His conclusion was that the sluggard lacked judgment, because Solomon saw that thorns had come up everywhere, the ground was covered with weeds, and the stone wall was in ruins. The sluggard clearly was not doing any work. Solomon seems to shake his head and repeat the same words in verses 33–34 that he declared in Proverbs 6:10–11.

If you have a lazy, undisciplined attitude when it comes to your finances, it will show in your "field." Things will be in disarray and the twins of poverty and scarcity can be expected to show up soon.

Discernment is first, discipline is second. Discipline fundamentally relates to *planning ahead*.

Three Principles of Savings:

3. Continue by Displaying Diligence
The third savings principle is this: *If you are going to save you must have diligence.* Proverbs again is rich with encouragement and warning. Proverbs 21:5 says:

The plans of the diligent lead to profit as surely as haste leads to poverty.

One who is focused and moving ahead should expect to see profit. Haste leading to poverty should remind you of our discussion about looking at yourself to see if you might have a debt problem. If you're the kind of person who falls for the get-rich-quick schemes, Solomon might be talking about you in this verse. Opportunities that require quick decisions—"Act now! Limited time only for those who move immediately!"—more than likely are too good to be true. If you want to find a way to be profitable, then you need to be diligent.

How diligent? Continue over weeks, months, and years. You grow it gradually, according to Proverbs 13:11b:

he who gathers money little by little makes it grow

Wow, that takes focus. That takes effort. That takes diligence. The principle of diligence really ties to the stewardship concept of *moving ahead*. All three principles, discernment (looking ahead), discipline (planning ahead) and diligence (moving ahead) are needed for you to be able to get to a place where you can save.

The First Steps

So how do you do it?

Before you do anything, you must make up your mind that you're going to do it *now*. When should you start saving? Now. *First* take stock of your herds and your flocks to find out where your money is going and the places that you can cut back on your expenses. *Then* you take the money that you have cut from your S^3 plan and honor God with it, building up to 10 percent. *Then* begin to save and invest at whatever level you can afford, but eventually work your way up to a place where you are saving 20 percent. One of the reasons behind saving 20 percent is that at that level you will see a drastic reduction in your consumption, which helps you with your contentment. It also provides resources for the current, former, and future generations, which is pleasing to God.

Three Practices of Savings:

1. Pay It before You See It

Here are three practices that will help you to save now. The first is *Pay it before you see it.* If you're the kind of person who has the tendency to spend money if you have access to more money, then pay it (to yourself) before you see it. What am I talking about? For example, participate in an employee 401K plan at work. Let your employer take say 5 percent (hopefully with some kind of employer match) out of your check as a payroll deduction. You never see it so you don't spend it. You could also set up automatic deductions that go directly to your savings account. (The good news is you can access that money quickly in case of an emergency. The bad news is that you may think a shoe sale at Bloomingdales is an emergency!)

Before I entered full-time in ministry, I used to have 5 percent deducted for my 401k contribution. Over the years I did not even think about it much. I only thought about the money that was being deducted when I saw my quarterly statements.

Three Practices of Savings:

2. Spread It before You Move It.

The second practice is *"Spread it before you move it."* You have always heard that you should diversify your investments, right? That is what Solomon is recommending in Ecclesiastes 11:1–2:

> **Cast your bread upon the waters, for after many days you will find it again.**
>
> **Give portions to seven, yes to eight, for you do not know what disaster may come upon the land.**

In verse 6, Solomon emphasizes the same principle in a different way:

> **Sow your seed in the morning, and at evening let not your hands be idle, for you do not know which will succeed, whether this or that, or whether both will do equally well.**

Solomon is saying that you do not know what is going to happen in life (see also Ecclesiastes 10:14), so make sure you do not put all your eggs in one basket. Think about the employees who invested all of their resources in their companies and watched their retirement go up in smoke when the company failed (e.g., Enron). Before you start to move any of your money, you need to spread it over several investments. You may think that the Charles Schwabs and the Fidelity

Investments of the world invented that financial principle, but it is actually biblical wisdom.

An investment in a mutual fund accomplishes this goal. The fund manager takes all the individual contributions and invests in a broad range of companies via equity or debt. If certain companies have tough stretches, others may do well and more than balance it out so that you can still achieve a positive return. If the money were only invested in one company, you would have to rise and fall on that company alone. Multiple investments spread the risk.

Three Practices of Savings:

3. Grow It before You Blow It.

The third practice I want you to grasp is *"Grow it before you blow it."* The Rothschild family was one of the wealthiest families in twentieth-century America. Someone once asked Baron Rothschild if he had ever seen any of the Seven Wonders of the World. And his reply was, "No, I haven't seen the Seven Wonders of the World, but I do know what the eighth wonder of the world is—compound interest." The best thing you can do is start saving and investing *today*. Today is better than tomorrow. Why? Because the sooner you let time start to work on your money, the more money you will have in the future. Time, interest rate, and risk are the three fundamental investment factors, but we're just going to focus on time right now. Your principle will grow through compounding interest.

Imagine that you want to retire at age sixty-five. (Who doesn't?) What if you invested $1,000 a year, every year until you reach your targeted retirement age? That's not a lot It's less than $3 a day. You can save that by simply passing up a tall premium coffee drink at Starbucks every day. Let's invest it in something that yields a 10 percent annual return. (Historically the stock market has posted a nominal return of well over 10 percent for the last several decades, so 10 percent seems reasonable and achievable. You just have to ride out the downturns and not remove all your stock investments while the money is in decline. Be able to stay for the long term—at least ten years).

Now, if you started investing that $1,000 per year (earning a 10 percent return) when you were twenty-five, forty years later when you reached retirement, you would have *$470,000*. Not huge money every year, but little by little (Proverbs 13:11) a total investment of $40,000 ($1,000 x 40 years) grows into a nice sum.

Time works on your money. You and I must start saving NOW, and more importantly we have to teach our kids to start doing it now.

Now let's say that you didn't start investing at age twenty-five. Maybe you did not get the memo on investing for the future until you were thirty-five. That same $1,000 per year (earning a 10 percent return) will only yield you $180,000 when you retire at age sixty-five. The difference of just ten years reduced your total proceeds from $470,000 to $180,000 because you didn't put in $10,000 between the ages of twenty-five to thirty-five. If you wait until you are 45 to start investing $1,000 per year (earning a 10 percent return), you will only have $63,000 when you retire in twenty years. So the $20,000 you could have invested between ages twenty-five and forty-five cost you $407,000 ($470,000 down to $63,000). That is the power of compound interest that Baron Rothschild called the eighth wonder of the world. Time works on your money.

You and I must start saving NOW, and more importantly we have to teach our kids to start doing it now. You might say, "I'm already thirty-five, forty-five, or fifty-five, so it's too late." Okay, you can only do what you can do. A thousand dollars a year, a premium cup of coffee a day. That's how I want you to think of it. If you give that up and just remain steady and diligent, little by little, your money will grow. It still will add up.

I am not living what I don't know. I was a senior partner at a real estate private equity firm for nine and one-half years. I looked at the total amount of money that I earned while I was there. Then I looked at how much money I saved and invested during that time. Since I was a partner, I had a share in all of our funds, and I was required to fund my portion of the capital that the investors expected our management team to put into our investments. Basically, that meant my annual compensation, above my living expenses and tithes, went toward meeting that obligation. Early on I had to borrow some money from my Dad to accomplish that task. I also used my home's line of credit. Once you subtract those borrowed amounts, I saved and invested 22 percent of my money (including 401k contributions and variable life insurance investments). Because I have done that, I was able to leave my firm for full-time ministry with the expectation that those investments that I have sown will reap a harvest over the next ten to twelve years that will allow me to take care of my family and continue to do the work of the kingdom.

Three Priorities of Savings:

1. Build Short- and Long-Term Savings

We have discussed three savings and investing principles and also three practices. Now let's turn our attention to three priorities. The first priority is that *you have to build short-term and long-term savings*. Develop the short-term savings by building a six-month emergency fund. That fund is set aside as cash in the bank (or a money-market account) and holds six months of your budgeted expenses. You do not put this money at risk for movement in the markets. Otherwise your money could be reduced by a market downturn at the same time that you have to liquidate to meet an emergency situation. In that case, you would not have the opportunity see recovery on the portion that you have withdrawn. I know very few people who actually have a six-month emergency fund, but at some point, you will need it because eventually you will have an emergency! At least begin by saving up a three-month emergency fund.

You also need long-term savings. Remember, we need to save for the former generation, the current generation, and the future generation. Recall that many of us are in the so-called sandwich generation, supporting and caring for parents as well as children. God will not be pleased with us if we don't repay (I Timothy 5:4) our parents and grandparents who've gone on before us and made a way for us to be in the position to earn and do well for ourselves. The Bible also reminds us that parents should lay up for the children (2 Corinthians 12:14). So long-term savings is for elder support, retirement, and inheritance. Build savings for both the short and long term and do it *now*.

Three Priorities of Savings:

2. Understand Risk

The second priority is *you must understand risk*. Risk is the second fundamental investment factor (time and interest

134

rate are the others). There is a concept in corporate finance called the risk/reward curve. As you move along the curve and take more risk, you should expect to gain a greater return. Conversely, when you are offered a greater anticipated return on an investment, you should expect that it will come with greater risk. Risk really is a measure of variability. The greater the risk, the greater the swing around what the investment may return. In a very risky investment, you could make a great deal of money or lose everything.

The U.S. government delivers money at what is customarily considered a risk-free rate. Why is it risk-free? It is because the U.S. government has never defaulted on an interest or principal payment of any of its obligations so that's about as safe as you can get. If you were to invest in U.S. treasuries with a ten-year, twenty-year or thirty-year maturity, you should expect to receive anywhere from a 2.3 to 3.4 percent return on your money (October, 2011) without taking any risk. Now, if somebody comes along to you and tells you that they'll give you a return on your money of 20 or 25 percent over the same time horizon, you'd better know that you are definitely taking some risk. And if you take the risk, you should get the reward, but you must understand that principle.

Suppose you have the opportunity to buy shares in a start-up oil-drilling company in Texas. The company projections show you can earn a 600 percent return on your money. Just know that it is oil-drilling. You can make a whole lot of money if you hit oil, or you can lose everything if the company has nothing but dry wells. There is a great deal of variability in that projected return, so do not just be enamoured with the return that you are expected to receive; understand as well the risk that you're taking.

Ultimately, this helps us avoid extremely risky investments like get-rich-quick schemes. If anybody is promising you huge returns that are characterized as practically guaranteed, your antenna should immediately go up. When you understand that risk-free or guaranteed really is a U.S. government return and somebody is offering you guaranteed returns that are a lot more than that, check the hype (and, as Public Enemy would say "Don't Believe the Hype!").

For those funds that you are going to need right away for your living expenses, do not take any risk. The longer your investment horizon, the more risk you can take.

Now there are relatively safe investments that investment-grade companies offer that yield a little more than U.S. government notes. (e.g., bank certificates of deposit, guaranteed investment contracts from insurance companies, or corporate bonds). These will provide a return a little higher than the corresponding U.S. bond or note as they are considered a little higher than risk-free. That's why rating agencies (like Standard & Poors or Moody's) evaluate company obligations and assign, for instance, a AAA rating to the strongest companies. These kinds of rating are designed to help investors understand risk. You need to understand risk as well.

There are investment funds with which you can take greater risk, and others that offer little risk. It just depends on your investment horizon. For those funds that you are going to need right away (that six-month emergency fund) for your living expenses, don't take any risk with those. The longer your investment horizon, the more risk you can take. The question is when do you expect to tap into the funds? Are these funds for your child to go to college? Good. If your child is sixteen, you will need those funds soon, so investments that preserve the capital are in order. If your child is two, you can afford to be more aggressive in taking risks, knowing that if there is a downturn with your investment, you still have time to recover.

Three Priorities of Savings:

3. Count the Cost

The third priority is *you have to count the cost*. Jesus said:

> **28 "Suppose one of you wants to build a tower. Will he not first sit down and estimate the cost to see if he has enough money to complete it? 29 For if he lays the foundation and is not able to finish it, everyone who sees it will ridicule him, 30 saying, `This fellow began to build and was not able to finish.' 31 "Or suppose a king is about to go to war against another king. Will he not first sit down and consider whether he is able with ten thousand men to oppose the one coming against him with twenty thousand? 32 If he is not able, he will send a delegation while the other is still a long way off and will ask for terms of peace (Luke 14:28–32)**

Jesus specifically was addressing the cost of discipleship, but His words certainly apply to the broader principle of contemplation before commitment. In both instances, the builder and the king need to stop and consider if they can truly follow through successfully on what is started. We must do the same when it comes to considering the cost associated with each investment we make.

It may sound like a great idea for you and a couple of friends to buy, rehab, and then sell houses. That is a great opportunity for somebody who has the time, energy, and skill set to deal with the physical and financial challenges of that business. Someone would also need to have sufficient cash flow to wait out any pricing or liquidity downturns that may occur in the housing market. In short, these "flips" don't always work the way you think they will, and you have to be patient. You must count costs, not only in terms of your time and returns, but the people aspect is also critical. Many good friendships have been ruined because people decided that they wanted to make money together. If you have a friend who is usually late for work, constantly complains about his working conditions, and performs his responsibilities with mediocrity, you may not want to start a business with that individual no matter how close you are and much fun you think it might be.

What about your time? There are always advertisements in the newspaper or on billboards that claim that you can make $100,000 a year, *in your spare time*. Beloved, I've never known anybody to make $100,000 in their spare time, unless they had two million dollars in the bank and were receiving 5 percent interest on it (now that's the way to make $100,000 in your spare time!) But other than that, you cannot make $100,000 in your spare time. Anything you do, you are going to have to work at it and you have to understand the time commitment. It takes time and energy to earn money. The more sweat equity you put into something, the more time and attention, the more you should expect to see some fruit. But you must always count the costs.

Three Problems in Savings:

1. You Cannot Truly Save Unless You Give to God

Now let's move on to three problems associated with savings and investing. Jesus sounds a key warning when it comes to saving and acquiring:

> **15"Watch out! Be on your guard against all kinds of greed; a man's life does not consist in the abundance of his possessions." 16 And he told them this parable: "The ground of a certain rich man produced a good crop. 17 He thought to himself, `What shall I do? I have no place to store my crops.' 18 "Then he said, `This is what I'll do. I will tear down my barns and build bigger ones, and there I will store all my grain and my goods. 19 And I'll say to myself, "You have plenty of good things laid up for many years. Take life easy; eat, drink and be merry." ' 20 "But God said to him, `You fool! This very night your life will be demanded from you. Then who will get what you have prepared for yourself?' 21 "This is how it will be with anyone who stores up things for himself but is not rich toward God." (Luke 12:15–21)**

Jesus starts out in verse 15 by warning His listeners to beware of all kinds of greed; then He affirms that a man's *self-worth* is not dictated by his *net worth*. No matter how much we know and understand the truth that Jesus proclaims in this verse, we still often attribute greater worth to people that have more money. We assume that they must be living better and cleaner lives and that God must love them more. We often say, "Why doesn't God love me, like He loves her? Why is he driving that and I'm driving this? Why can't God love me like He loves Oprah? He must really love Oprah Winfrey a lot!" Well, He does love Oprah a lot, but He loves you just as much as He loves her (John 3:16).

There are many reasons that you cannot make a direct correlation between what a person has and the condition of their spiritual life. In fact, often that is an inverted relationship. Many people who are successful in this life won't be successful in the next because they haven't laid up any treasure in the next. You cannot take it with you, so you must send it on ahead by investing in the kingdom and in God's people.

Jesus then tells a parable about a certain rich man to emphasize His point. This man thought that the way to deal with his ever-increasing goods was to tear down his barns and build bigger ones. That way he could take life easy, eat, drink, and be merry. But God said that a man like that is a fool. Verse 21 reveals why he is a fool: he stored up things for himself but was not rich toward God.

The problem was *not* that he was saving. He was. But Jesus reveals that *you cannot truly save unless you give*. This is a biblical principle. You should give to God first and then focus on saving. If you don't, you are a fool! Here was a man who was not rich toward God. He did not honor Him with his possessions. He obviously did not practice the guiding biblical principle of tithing. He gave only to himself.

Some people have the savings part down. They are always saving. They have an emergency fund. They have sufficient long-term savings. They have investments that will take care of the current and future needs of their families—but they do not give anything to the kingdom of God. They are fools, God says (verse 20). If you have that problem, then you need to rectify it because God is not pleased with those people that save and don't give. You have to stop greed first by allocating 0 percent to debt, and next sow to God by giving 10 percent. *Then* it is appropriate to save for your goals with 20 percent of your money going to savings/investments. However, if you are saving and not giving, watch out.

The size of the rich man's barns was not the problem. If you are honoring God with your resources, you should actually look forward to a barn "problem" (Proverbs 3:9-10). But let's do the first things first. If you treat God like He is leftovers and not first fruits, you're robbing Him. You are not robbing Him of money; you are robbing Him of *glory* (Isaiah 42:8). If I were you, I would stop my savings program, and start focusing on my giving program. I am not necessarily suggesting that you stop the contributions to your 401k, but you should not allocate additional resources to bigger savings accounts when you have not honored God appropriately. As additional resources come in (whether new growth or expense savings), you need to funnel those monies into kingdom building not barn building.

Three Problems in Savings:

2. Focusing on Getting Rich

The second problem to look out for is *a focus on getting rich*. If while saving, getting rich becomes your all-out pursuit, you will have a major problem. As Paul warned,

> **9 People who want to get rich fall into temptation and a trap and into many foolish and harmful desires that plunge men into ruin and destruction. 10 For the love of money is a root of all kinds of evil. Some people, eager for money, have wandered from the faith and pierced themselves with many griefs.** (1 Timothy 6:9–11)

You can't have as a major goal in your life to get rich. You just can't. The Bible tells us that we must always seek the spiritual before the material (Matthew 6:33). But if you want to focus on the material you are opening yourself up to many difficulties. Verse 9 could not make it any more plain: ruin and destruction accompany those that take the path of wanting to get rich. We must not hoard our money and try to fatten our savings accounts.

Now, I am not saying that God doesn't want you to be ambitious or excellent in all that you do. The *love* of money is the problem, not the money itself. As we have been reminded, money is to be used not abused, used not wasted and used not served. Clearly, it is to be used. You and I are called to use money and love people, not to love money and use people.

If money becomes your all-out pursuit, you will get that and nothing else. And is it really worth it? Jesus said the soul is worth far more than anything the world offers (Luke 9:25) and He described the wide gate and broad road that leads to destruction (Matthew 7:13). I can assure you there is not a big flashing sign at the entrance that says, "Come on down, this road leads straight to hell. Destruction, pain, grief and eternal damnation await you." If there was a sign advertising that result, I am sure less people would travel that road.

Instead, Satan is a master at hiding the end result from you. He loves to show you the festivities of drinking out with your friends, without showing you the DUI conviction and the 3 a.m. clutching of the toilet bowl. He loves to entice you with the casual sexual encounter without showing you the sexually transmitted disease you get to keep forever like luggage. Satan is always promoting self-deception. Christ is always promoting self-denial.

Money is no different. Satan loves to show you the corner office without revealing the emptiness and vanity that often accompany increased possessions. Some of the most miserable people I know are rich. Some of the most satisfied and happy people I know have very modest resources. Paul is warning there is a deceptive road you can travel with the pursuit and love of money. At the end you often get much less than anticipated.

Three Problems in Savings:

3. Looking toward Gambling

The third problem we may face is the temptation to gamble. *You should not gamble.*

Oh my, is he going to talk about the lottery? Yes, he is! Is he going to talk about the river boat? Yes, he is! Let's begin with the bottom line: The lottery is *not* a savings plan or an investment plan. You do not increase your allocation of lottery tickets as you get more resources!

I know you like to tell yourself that you are just playing the lottery or the riverboat slot machines or card games for entertainment, but the truth is you are being wasteful. As stewards, you and I should not be gambling. That is the very essence of a get-rich quick scheme: attempting to get something for nothing. It does not matter if you trying to fill your savings account with the proceeds. (You may actually deplete your savings if you're not careful.)

That goes for casino games as well. All casino games are designed to take your money. Even if you are winning, stay long enough and you will give it all back and then some. Time is on the casino's side, that is why there are no windows and clocks in those places. They do not want you to make any connection to how long you have been there. There are better ways for God's people to entertain themselves that do not have the hazards of gambling.

The real problem with gambling is it can get away from you. It'll start there, but it's like being on an escalator. You keep moving up, and then the rush that you feel from winning the lottery isn't enough, so you want to take that feeling and "double down" on it by going to the river boat. The next thing you know, you are taking annual trips to Vegas, and you are losing quite a bit of money. Now, there is something that the enemy would love to see happen. He would love to see you waste God's resources on foolishness and compromise your testimony.

"Come on pastor, are you saying I can't even buy a square in the Super Bowl office pool or fill out a NCAA March Madness bracket for ten dollars? Those activities are not necessarily harmful to your testimony, but I would not think of it that way. Those are times that you could make a statement by *not* blending in with the crowd but standing different from the crowd. That would actually be *helpful* to your testimony. You could use that opportunity to explain stewardship principles to those that would inquire. I know, it sounds serious. It is – and what you do is between you and your Lord.

Three Pursuits for Your Money:

1. Seek to Care of Your Family

Last but not least, I want to give you three pursuits. The pursuits are in concert with the concept of saving 20 percent for goals. The first pursuit we have already talked about it. *You must take care of your family.* Your pursuit should not be to get rich (2 Timothy 6:9–10) but you definitely seek to make provision for your loved ones. Again, there is nothing wrong with being ambitious, striving for excellence and being diligent in your career efforts. However the focus cannot be to get rich or die trying (no offense 50 Cent). Keep things in the proper perspective. (What really helps you and I keep things on the proper perspective is to give before we save.) Scripture tells us over and over to take care of our families. It's about people, not things.

Three Pursuits for Your Money:

2. Become Financially Free

The second pursuit is to *become financially free so that you can serve the Lord.* If you spend many years sowing and sowing with diligence, limiting your consumption and operating with contentment, at some point you should see some results, right? There should be a time to reap (Ecclesiastes 3:2), and when that happens you will hopefully be able to generate more choices for yourself. For instance, if you have been working two jobs, now you can only work one. That will free up more of your time. So what are you going to do with more time? Lay around on the couch and do nothing? No. Now that you have more time, you have a greater ability to pour into your family and also accomplish kingdom work through ministry. Remember, stewardship is everything in your life—time, talent and treasure. God wants to be honored with all, and He deserves to be.

As I mentioned, I retired from a private equity firm at age forty after being a partner for over nine years. I had invested in our real estate funds and expect to receive a return in the future as these funds mature. At the same time I worked downtown, I served as the senior pastor of a newly planted church for the last of those five years. The Lord moved me to leave my downtown job and serve Him full-time in ministry. It was a *very* difficult decision for several reasons. The uncertainty of the future weighed heavily on my mind. (Will what has been stored up be enough?) Also, I have always, like most men, identified who I am very closely with the job I held. I would no longer be a senior vice president of a prestigious firm, but a simple pastor of a small church in the Chicago suburbs. Could I handle that?

The Lord helped me to move past those questions and I followed His prompting and left my job.

And guess what? The immediate financial blessing I received when I left was more than I could have imagined. God used the head of the firm to encourage me by sending me out the door with a sum of money that eased my mind about the future (come on somebody!) and let me know that God was going to take care of me and my family. God brought me to a place where He impressed upon me that He has something else for me to do besides pursue riches for riches sake. Trust me, I could have just stayed where I was and made real money. The hard work was done. I had enough experience to be able to handle the work of managing people, process, and projects, and I had climbed the corporate ladder to a comfortable rung at the top. This is where you dream of getting in your career. From where I was, you can really start to pile up some serious resources as you finish up the "back nine" of your career.

But that's not what God had for me. God said, "No, I want you to take a different path." And when He told me that years ago, I said, "Yes Lord, I'm available to you." I did not know what it would mean but now He is walking me through it. It has been almost five years now and I can testify that God has been good. Even in this recessionary economy, God has shown Himself strong, and I know He will continue to provide for me and my family while I do His work. So I'm living this thing.

Get to a point where more, as nice as it might be, is not as appealing as being obedient to what God says.

Now you cannot make a decision like the one I made without a good measure of contentment. You have to get to a point where more, as nice as it might be, is not as appealing as being obedient to what God says. Getting a taste of wealth is difficult because the higher you climb, the nicer it gets and you stop looking at where you've come from, and start looking only at where you can go. In order to get "there" a few more million (remember John D. Rockefeller) sure would be nice.

At the time God told me to leave Greenfield Partners, the firm was raising two more investment funds, the largest amount of money raised since the firm started (almost $2 billion dollars). If I would have stayed around for just one or two more years, I would have had an interest in those funds. Those investments would have represented more resources to me in the future and presumably more security. A few of my close friends at the firm who knew I was going to leave, begged me to stay one more year at least because there were millions at stake. I had to tell them I could not stay because God said it was time to go.

I told myself (and those friends) whatever has been laid up to this point would have to be enough. You cannot turn down the opportunity to get more if you are not content. Given the choice between moving on to the next level (as attractive as that is!) or staying where I am and moving away from my downtown job so I can be obedient to what God told me, I chose the latter. And I bear witness to the Scripture in I Timothy 6:6 that says godliness with contentment is great gain!

Three Pursuits for Your Money:

3. Give Away More and More

The third pursuit that you and I must undertake is to *start giving away more and more*. I would love for us all to collectively get to a place where we have a heart of contentment. In that place we could conclude that we are comfortable with our standard of living and instead of building any bigger barns, we would just decide to give away more. Pastor Rick Warren, who wrote the book *A Purpose-Driven Life,* said that he has become a reverse tither. He gives away 90 percent of his money, and only keeps 10 pecent. That's what's up! I'm trying to get there.

When you're comfortable with where God has you, and you have made provision to take care of your family, you can decide to increase your giving above the 10 percent tithe. If you're in constant communication with your God, you'll know when it's right for you. I'm not supposed to judge it and nobody else is supposed to judge it for you. You decide with God how that will work, but at some point, enough is enough. You need to draw a line in the sand and say, "As I get more, I'll give more of it away."

Think about if somebody has a particular need in your family or in the community of faith, and you have actually been saving 20 percent of your money. Doesn't it become a little easier to make a decision to give something if you actually have something to give? It makes those decisions less stressful. The more you actually save and invest, the more you can actually take care of your family and give to the kingdom work. That giving will take the form of not only money but also time, as you free yourself up to serve Him as you become financially free.

Discussion Questions:

1. Think about the three practices: Pay it before you see it, spread it before you move it and grow it before you blow it. Are these principles hard to do in America's culture?
2. Think about the three priorities: You have to build short-term and long-term savings, you must understand risk, and you have to count the cost. Are you ready to invest? Do you have more questions about investing? What are some steps you can take to begin investing?
3. Think about the three problems: You cannot save unless you give, you should not focus on getting rich, and you should not gamble. Do you have a problem in any of these areas? What do you need to do in order to take precautions against these problems?
4. Think about the three pursuits: You must take care of your family, become financially free so that you can serve the Lord, and start giving away more and more. Does it make sense that the more financially secure you become, the freer you are to give? How would you serve the Lord through financial freedom? What will be your steps towards that freedom?

CHAPTER 7:
DO THE RIGHT THING

How to Allocate Your Money

0%, is our allocation to debt in order to stop greed.
10% goes to giving because we need to sow to God.
20% is targeted for savings/investing so that we might save for goals.

30% is set aside for taxes, so we can support the government.

40% is left for consumption so that we can satisfy with goods.

You may recall that Spike Lee movie *Do the Right Thing*. In one scene Mookie (played by Lee) is on his way to work when "Da Mayor" stops him and says, "Mookie, I got something to tell you."

"Hurry up, Mayor," Mookie answers. "I'm trying to go to work."

Da Mayor is known for being long-winded, so Mookie anticipates he will be held up for a while, but he must show him respect since he is an older man.

"Doctor, always do the right thing." Da Mayor says.

"Is that it?' Mookie asks.

"That's it."

Mookie is relieved and says, "I've got it. I'm gone."

When it comes to the fourth allocation of our money recipe 30 percent to taxes in order to support the federal government— it's all about you and I doing the right thing.

A question may already be on your mind—why 30 percent for taxes? This is an average—consider the 30 percent a place-holder, if you will, because everybody is not going to pay 30 percent in taxes. Some will pay less and others (painfully) will pay more (up to 35 percent for 2011 federal income tax). So whatever it is, it is (but 30 percent is a good round number and it helps our resource recipe flow nicely!).

Doing the Right Thing:
Submit to Governing Authority

However, you and I need to understand *why* we need to do *what* we need to do. Romans 13 is a pivotal passage that helps us understand our responsibilities to the government. So, let's make sure that we have a good understanding of this passage as it relates to what God says is the right thing to do. Romans 13:1–7 says:

> **1 Everyone must submit himself to the governing authorities, for there is no authority except that which God has established. The authorities that exist have been established by God. 2 Consequently, he who rebels against the authority is rebelling against what God has instituted, and those who do so will bring judgment on themselves. 3 For rulers hold no terror for those who do right, but for those who do wrong. Do you want to be free from fear of the one in authority? Then do what is right and he will commend you. 4 For he is God's servant to do you good. But if you do wrong, be afraid, for he does**

not bear the sword for nothing. He is God's servant, an agent of wrath to bring punishment on the wrongdoer. 5 Therefore, it is necessary to submit to the authorities, not only because of possible punishment but also because of conscience. 6 This is also why you pay taxes, for the authorities are God's servants, who give their full time to governing. 7 Give everyone what you owe him: If you owe taxes, pay taxes; if revenue, then revenue; if respect, then respect; if honor, then honor.

The apostle Paul's words here really hearken back to Romans 12: 1–2, where he encourages us to *perform our worship, reform our ways,* and *transform our will.* Our interaction with the civil authorities is a practical expression of a life that truly is a living sacrifice, "holy and pleasing to God." Therefore, the first thing that you need to understand from this passage is God requires certain conduct by you (verse one).

What is the conduct required? Everyone must submit himself to the governing authorities. That word "submit" is the same word used in Scripture to describe the appropriate response of children to parents (including Jesus to His parents when He was a child), slaves to their masters, the church to Christ, wives to husbands and Christ to God the Father. The Greek word is *hupotasso,* and it is always used to signify subjection to a proper and recognized higher authority. *Hupotasso* literally means to bear up under or to place under.

You and I need to realize that we have been placed under governmental authority. Once we realize this truth, Paul is saying that we must conduct ourselves like those who recognize the authority that is in place above us. Further, there is no authority established except that which God has established.

You may say, "That statement can't be true because there are so many governments around the world that bring God no glory through their actions, abuse their powers, and cause their citizens to suffer." But even Satan's authority has been established by God. The temptation of Jesus by Satan in the desert reveals Satan's authority over the kingdoms of this world. Satan took Jesus to a high mountain, and Luke records that the devil

> **5 ...showed him in an instant all the kingdoms of the world. 6 And he said to him, "I will give you all their authority and splendor, for it has been given to me, and I can give it to anyone I want to. (Luke 4:5-6)**

Through the fall of man in the garden of Eden, Satan became the prince of this world (Ephesians 2:2, John 16:11, I John 5:19) and God has allowed him to operate until He returns to set things in order. He has a divine plan. The establishment of authorities in Romans 13 speaks to God's sovereignty and His control over His creation. Although we see governments operating in a flawed and fallen environment, I don't want you to conclude that our creator and the sustainer of all life is asleep at the wheel. He's not asleep at the wheel, despite what you see.

Everything that is going on God knows about. He is not caught off guard and He is not surprised by anything. In Daniel 4:17, in a passage where Daniel is interpreting a dream by King Nebuchadnezzar, Daniel says:

> **17 " `The decision is announced by messengers, the holy ones declare the verdict, so**

> **that the living may know that the Most High is sovereign over the kingdoms of men and gives them to anyone he wishes and sets over them the lowliest of men.'**

God is in control and one of His attributes is immanence, meaning He is actively involved in nature, human nature, and human history. The corruption we see in government due to the fall of man does not negate our responsibility to government, so you don't have an excuse as it relates to the conduct that is required.

However, God does allow room for you and me to do what the apostle Peter and the disciples did in Acts 5. The authorities ordered the apostles not to teach in Jesus' name, but Peter and the other apostles replied that they must obey God rather than men (Acts 5:29). If there comes a time when governmental authorities attempt to have us do things that are against the revealed will of God, we must do the same. However, we must be prepared to suffer the consequences for our actions (Acts 5:40). Our expectation should be that we will face persecution when we obey God rather than men. If any Spirit-led objection is absent, the Scripture is clear here in Romans that you must subject yourself to the recognized, God-ordained authority in government. That is the conduct that is required by you.

Doing the Right Thing:
Reject Authority and Expect Consequences

Romans 13:2 reveals that we can expect consequences when we reject authority. If you and I do not do the right thing as it relates to civil authorities, we are bringing judgment upon ourselves. Why? Because these powers were instituted by God.

God is the one to whom we must one day answer for our interactions with government.

According to Romans 13:3-4, government should fundamentally commend those who do good and punish those who do wrong. I realize that is holding government to a very high expectation, and we are no doubt not going to see it executed flawlessly. First of all, we would have to presume that governments could understand what is right and what is wrong. The Bible is our guide to understand and arbitrate right from wrong and no government bases its policies purely on God's Word.

The best form of government that has been created is not democracy, oligarchy, monarchy or dictatorship. The best government that we have seen is theocracy (rule by God—and it is coming back when Jesus returns!). Theocracy is the best form of government because God knows best. The children of Israel had a theocracy, but they wanted a human king (1 Samuel 8). But America does not have a theocracy, so we have to work with what we have. However, the concept of government that God has revealed is that a government should be God's servant to do you good if you do what is right. Government should also be God's servant as an agent of wrath to punish you if you do wrong.

What about a *Bad* Government?

You might think that since we do not have a theocracy that you can opt out of your responsibility and the conduct required because you do not like the government we have. You may not like the president, the Congress, or any of the state or municipal leaders that we have, so you may feel justified in choosing not to listen to or submit to them. Well, that's not how Romans 13 is saying that we should respond.

Understand that Paul is writing to Christians in Rome while Nero is the emperor. In just a few years after these words are penned, Nero begins the wholesale persecution of Christians throughout Rome (reportedly in AD 64). Those believers who faced that wrath could no doubt affirm that they did nothing to deserve punishment and that Nero's government was not good to those who were good. Nevertheless, the *concept* of government is still pure and God has chosen to govern the world through the authorities that have been established.

You cannot throw out an institution that God has established just because your personal experience with it is bad. God established marriage as an institution. The fact that we have seen so many failed marriages should not lead us to the conclusion that the *institution* is bad, but only that the *execution* is bad. The same can be said for our church experience. We know that shepherds are supposed to feed and care for the flock (see Ezekiel 34). Just because we have seen pastors that have abused their influence and taken advantage of the sheep does not mean the institution of the church is bad, only that we have seen poor execution of what God established.

Bottom line: We do not have the right to opt out because we see poor execution. What we should do, particularly as it relates to government, is to support and bring in those who can execute the concept of government as God has revealed it. I believe those who are Christians should be able to do that better than anybody. Believers should be able to understand the concept of government and seek counsel for its execution from the one who created it, which is God. When you have a problem with an appliance in your house, what do you usually do? Okay, you probably hit it, kick it, or punch it, so let me backtrack. What *should* you do? If you still have the manual that came with the appliance, you go back to it in order to figure out what went wrong. Through the manual, the original equipment manufacturer (OEM) has told you everything that you need to know about the operation and maintenance of this appliance.

The OEM sometimes even includes a trouble-shooting guide and frequently asked questions, which anticipate common problems that may arise with the use of the equipment. As the OEM of government, God desires that we come back to Him to get government right because He is the one who established government.

Having a Good Conscience

According to Romans 13:5, we should submit not just to avoid trouble (including possible punishment) but also to have a good conscience. God wants to raise your level of awareness as to what He is trying to accomplish, and He wants you to get with the program and do the right thing. Punishment is always an immediate motivator—that is why you and I hopefully don't speed down the highway at 100 miles an hour. However, if we knew that there was a stretch of road where there were no cops, many of us would go as fast as we wanted; The fear of punishment would be absent, and our obligation to do what is right would be tested—and often compromised.

Now, there are a lot of things that you can probably get away with, but God is saying that He does not want your submission to be based upon whether or not you think you can get away with it, but because you want to do the right thing. Conscience should be the motivation to subject yourself to the higher authorities.

Pay Your Taxes

Paul gets specific in verse 6 about our obedience to the government authorities: We must pay to them our taxes.

Why should we pay? First, the agents of government are God's servants. Second, those agents devote their full time to doing their jobs. This is reminiscent of Paul's affirmation that those who preach the gospel should make their living from the gospel (1 Corinthians 9:14). Here Paul tells us that those who are governing full time should derive their support from the people they govern. Although I am sure we could list the myriad of things that we know that the government is not doing, there is no doubt more things that the government *is* doing. Also, as much as we would like to complain, we actually have it pretty good right where we are. Would you want to live in another country? I wouldn't. Name another country that you would rather be in, taking into account their form of government and how its officials administer it.

There is so much that is done that we take for granted. For instance, you know that once a week when you set your trash out, the next morning someone comes to take it away. If you live in a cold weather area like Chicago, when you see the news at night and a tremendous overnight snowfall is forecast, your expectation is that the snow will be removed and the streets salted. That is what we expect because we're paying for it. But the apostle Paul helps us to remember that there are people who give their full-time focus to making it all work. For that effort, we need to pay our taxes. Taxes express our support of the government and the services it provides.

Beyond the Money: Paying Respect to Leaders

As we turn our attention to verse 7, we get to the heart of the matter. "Give everyone what you owe him." And in order to make it clear so that there is no confusion, Paul is telling us that if you owe taxes, then pay taxes; if its revenue, then pay revenue; if it is respect, then pay respect. That is all a part of recognizing the authority over you and submitting to it. It is not just with your checkbook, although Paul includes that because he speaks specifically of taxes and revenue. But it is also about respect and honor as you understand the concept of government. Now, there is room for disagreement with governmental policies. We can be involved in efforts to change the way things are done, but we need to work within the system and its restraints.

For instance, as those that support a pro-life position (which I hope we all understand is the correct Biblical position since it honors life that God has ordained and values), we should be working to transform the hearts and minds of those around us. The choice is *always* life. In the hierarchy of human values, life is always at the top. So as we seek to encourage other folks to understand that, it would be perfectly acceptable to stand in front of an abortion clinic to hand out literature, or try to persuade someone to find other ways to deal with the circumstances they face. That would be within the realms and the boundaries of the laws that have been set up. What would *not* be acceptable is to somehow sneak a backpack into the clinic that contains an incendiary device and blow up four doctors and six patients that are inside. You cannot do that. Why? Because that's murder and that reduces you to a level where no one should go. (And, ironically, you would have devalued adult human life even as you seek to value unborn human life!)

You should then expect the sword of the government, and right soon. If you do not like something, you work for change within the system.

And so the commandment is to "give everyone what you owe him." Now, I do not want you to think that "give" in this instance is a suggestion. It is a commandment. And the word "give" is not the usual word that is translated from the Greek word *didomai*. It is the Greek word *apodidomai*. The difference between the two words is the first means to give and the second really means to give back. Give because you have received. There is recognition that you have an obligation in place and that you must address it by giving back. It is the same word translated as 'repaying' in I Timothy 5:4:

> **"But if a widow has children or grandchildren, these should learn first of all to put their religion into practice by caring for their own family and so *repaying* their parents and grandparents, for this is pleasing to God"** (*emphasis mine*).

Give because there is an obligation in place to those who govern full time as authorities. They have been established by God.

The idea is not give to your parents because it's a nice thing to do. No, give back to them because you owe them. There is a different weight to these words once you understand that you are to give because there is an obligation in place. Obligation to whom? Those who govern full time as authorities that have been established by God. Your conscience requires that you submit so give what you owe.

In Mark 12, the slick Pharisees came to Jesus and they said:

"Teacher, we know you are a man of integrity. You aren't swayed by men, because you pay no attention to who they are; but you teach the way of God in accordance with the truth. Is it right to pay taxes to Caesar or not? Should we pay or shouldn't we?" (vs. 14–15)

They knew that if they could get Jesus on record saying do not pay taxes, they could go straight to the Roman leaders and tell them that Jesus was out there messing with their government's money. They wanted to trap Him and cause Him trouble. But Jesus did not accommodate them. Mark reports,

But Jesus knew their hypocrisy. "Why are you trying to trap me?" he asked. "Bring me a denarius and let me look at it." 16 They brought the coin, and he asked them, "Whose portrait is this? And whose inscription?" "Caesar's," they replied. 17 Then Jesus said to them, "Give to Caesar what is Caesar's and to God what is God's." (vs. 15b-17)

The word "pay" that the Pharisees (15a) use concerning taxes is translated from the Greek work *didomai*. Jesus responded to them in verse 17 to *apodidomai* to Caesar what is Caesar's. In other words, give *back* to Caesar what he is owed. His image is on the coin, so give back to him what he is due.

But more importantly Jesus adds that they should give *back* to God what God is owed, also because of image. You were born and you were created in the *image* of God, so give Caesar the coin but give God your *life*! God wants you to give Him back your life—you owe it to Him.

So, *apodidomai* is giving in fulfilment of an obligation or expectation. Therefore, if you owe taxes, pay taxes. Now, does that mean that you should not be seeking every legitimate deduction? No, you should deduct everything that is available to you. You also might want to get a tax professional to help you because there may be deductions for which you qualify that you might not even know about.

When I was in graduate school studying for my MBA at Northwestern, I was in the school's four-quarter program. Usually it takes two years, or six quarters, to receive an MBA, with a summer break between the first and second years. But I was enrolled in the four-quarter program that was available to those who had graduated from an undergraduate business program. This program allowed you to complete the entire degree in one calendar year by exempting you out of two quarters worth of classes that you completed as part of your undergraduate business program. I received my degree in June and had already filed my tax return in April.

One of my classmates was selling T-shirts with the top ten reasons to go to the four-quarter program. Well, I looked at it and discovered that the number one reason listed was that the tuition of $36,000 was tax-deductible. WHAT???!!! I did not know anything about this being tax-deductible! I said, "Wait a minute, hold on, who made these T-shirts?" I found out it was a classmate whose father was a partner at Peat Marwick, a major accounting firm at the time. After talking to her, I discovered that because the degree was completed within one year, the costs qualified as un-reimbursed business expenses that related to education and were able to be deducted. So guess what I did? I filed a 1040X and we got back about $5,000 or $6,000!

As a matter of fact, several years later I ran into a high school friend who also graduated from the four-quarter program (he had been out two years). Apparently, they didn't make any T-shirts the year he graduated because he was in the dark, too! After I told him about it, he filed a 1040X and got his money back.

My advice: check the backs of all of your T-shirts and make sure you talk to people. You might be missing out on some money that is due you. But pay what you owe, and if you qualify for certain things, by all means avail yourself of those deductions. However, do not pretend that you have a home business, and then deduct the proportionate square footage of your phantom home office from your housing expenses as some kind of business deduction. Those are the kind of games that people play. God is not calling you to do that. He is calling you to be above reproach. He wants you to do the right thing.

Paul also says that if you owe revenue, then pay revenue. If you are supposed to get a municipal sticker for your car, then get one. If you have incurred parking tickets, then pay them. If you are supposed to pay a registration fee to have a pet, then pay it. Do not say that the city gets enough of your money and you are protesting. No, *whatever* you owe, you are supposed to pay. That is part of your Christian testimony to the world. Pay your taxes and fees.

Continuing in Romans 13, Paul writes:

8 Let no debt remain outstanding, except the continuing debt to love one another, for he who loves his fellowman has fulfilled the

> **law. 9 The commandments, "Do not commit adultery," "Do not murder," "Do not steal," "Do not covet," and whatever other commandment there may be, are summed up in this one rule: "Love your neighbor as yourself." 10 Love does no harm to its neighbor. Therefore love is the fulfillment of the law.**

The apostle Paul now calls on believers to submit to the government and complete their obligations to civil authorities for love's sake. Move past for punishment's sake even move past for conscience's sake—do it for *love's sake*.

The apostle continues to raise our motivation so that it can get to the highest motivation. He is saying do the right thing and do it for love. Do it because you need to love your neighbor as you love yourself. Do it because love does no harm to its neighbour and is the fulfilment of the law. Once you and I understand that love does no harm to its neighbor, then we will do the right thing as it relates to honoring the government that is in place above us. Do it for love.

Do the Right Thing Right Now

Finally, the apostle Paul calls his readers to immediate action:

> **11 And do this, understanding the present time. The hour has come for you to wake up from your slumber, because our salvation is nearer now than when we first believed. 12 The night is nearly over; the day is almost here. So let us put aside the deeds of darkness**

and put on the armor of light. 13 Let us behave decently, as in the daytime, not in orgies and drunkenness, not in sexual immorality and debauchery, not in dissension and jealousy. 14 Rather, clothe yourselves with the Lord Jesus Christ, and do not think about how to gratify the desires of the sinful nature. (vv. 11–14)

Paul is telling us to wake up, which means that not only do we need to do the right thing, but we need to do the right thing *right now*. He says it is high time to wake up because our salvation is nearer than when we believed. Every day that we keep living, the return of our Lord Jesus Christ draws nearer. Because of this truth, we should become more and more Christlike (2 Corinthians 3:18) as time goes on. The charge to us is: Don't just submit for punishment's sake, don't just do it for conscience's sake, don't even do it for love's sake. Beloved, do it for *Christ's sake*.

We must get to a place where we understand that all we do must be done for Christ's sake (Colossians 3:17). That is the highest and best motivation that will keep us regardless of the situation. This motivation will inspire us to action regardless of whether we are being watched or regardless of whether we think we can get away with what we've done. When we understand that now our salvation is nearer than when we believed, when we understand that we need to walk in light and not in darkness, and that we need to put on the Lord Jesus and make not provision for the flesh , we will *always* do the right thing.

Discussion Questions

1. Does the government sometimes annoy or anger you? Does knowing that God established authority, even Satan's authority, help you? How can you begin to trust God in the area of government?

2. Discuss the issue of taxes. Do you pay your taxes each year? Are you aware of all the deductions that might be available to you?

3. A commandment in Romans 13:7 is "Give everyone what you owe him." Do you follow this principle? Do you owe anything to anyone—be in financially or otherwise?

4. Romans 13 talks about four motivations (punishment, conscience, love, Christ). What are the right motivations? Are you motivated correctly in the way you treat your government and others? What are ways you might need to change in this area?

CHAPTER 8:
HOW THEN SHOULD WE LIVE?

magine you see a recipe for a certain dessert, and it calls for (among other things) two cups of sugar, two tablespoons of vanilla extract, and a cooking time of sixty minutes at 350 degrees. You decide that using a white granular substance like salt is just as good as using sugar and since vinegar also starts with a 'v' you will substitute that instead of vanilla extract. Lastly, you don't believe you have the time to wait sixty minutes for this dessert to bake so you decide to change the cooking time to thirty minutes and turn the oven up to 500 degrees. When you pull your new creation out of the oven it looks nothing like the picture you have but you are not dissuaded. You grab a fork and taste it only to experience a new low in disappointment. Are you surprised it is so awful? You should not be—you didn't follow the recipe!

The same is true for our spiritual lives. The Bible is our cookbook and contains all the recipes that we need in order to achieve successful outcomes for our lives. Sometimes we bristle at the instructions that we see and question the wisdom of God's recipes. When that happens, we attempt to substitute ingredients or change parameters in order to satisfy our particular desires. Our results are predictably unsatisfactory.

The area of finances is one where God is very clear about what it is He would have us to do. There is a recipe. It is also true that this area is one where many of us hesitate to follow what God has laid out. Now, if you move away from God's recipe on how you should handle your resources before Him, you should not be surprised when your finances are in chaos or do not look like you desire. <u>If you want the results of the recipe, then follow the recipe.</u>

In the area of personal finances, a lot of pain, suffering, and heartache can be avoided if folks would simply follow the recipe. Step by step we have spent time discussing a new money recipe that honors God: <u>0, 10, 20, 30, 40</u>.

0%, is our allocation to *debt* in order *to stop greed*.

10% goes to *giving* because we need to *sow to God*.

20% is targeted for *savings/investing* so that we might *save for goals*.

30% is set aside for *taxes*, so we can *support the government*.

40% is left for *consumption* so that we can *satisfy with goods*.

We haven't spent any time discussing the 40 percent for consumption. Guess what? We don't need to. I am of a firm mind that this recipe will work whether you make $40,000 per year or $400,000 per year. In America consumption is like the dog. But in God's economy, consumption is only the *tail* on the dog. As you know, the tail does not wag the dog, but the dog wags the tail. Therefore, we should focus on the four other active ingredients in our money recipe to reduce our consumption. Once the other pieces are in place, the consumption takes care of itself. If you are following the money recipe and consuming 40 percent of what you bring in, you are definitely getting a handle on greed and reinforcing the spiritual value of contentment.

An Honest Question

God told the prophet Ezekiel to repeat to the people of Israel their concern about how to live in light of their sins:

> **"O thou son of man, speak unto the house of Israel; Thus ye speak, saying, If our transgressions and our sins be upon us, and we pine away in them, how should we then live?" (Ezekiel 33:10, King James Version)**

It is a question we also can ask about our finances. If we are going to have the correct view of riches, *how should we then live?* The people had asked the prophet, "We know that we have been doing things wrong, but we need you to tell us, Ezekiel, how to live right. Our sins and my transgressions are weighing us down. How can we turn it around?"

This is an honest question that you must ask yourself as you look at your finances, and your whole life. Remember, stewardship is about more than just this treasure; it includes your talent and treasure too. It is your whole life, and God desires that you honor Him in every aspect.

Start with Correction

So the question is, *How should we then live*? I suggest that you and I do five things: correction of our mindset, reflection on eternity, selection for enjoyment, direction from God, and connection to others.

The first thing is that we should live our lives with *correction – not the world's way but God's way.* You and I have made mistakes in the past that have to be corrected and we must start now. It is unacceptable to say to God, "I've heard you but I'm going to get back to you on this later."

Correction of our mind-set is a critical first step. Our mind-set should be "Ignore the world's way and pursue God's way." Look at consumption the same way God looks at consumption. It is the tail on the dog. Consumption is not everything, although the American culture of immediate gratification would attempt to persuade you differently. As pilgrims passing through with a citizenship that is in heaven (Philippians 3:20), we must start to act like it. We must understand that what happens during our short life here, seventy years—or eighty, if we have the strength (Psalms 90:10), is the set up for our lives in eternity. This life is nothing but a drop in a bucket, therefore we must have a kingdom perspective for we are truly kingdom people.

Along the way we must be alert to Satan's temptations for us to compromise. Peter warns:

Be self-controlled and alert. Your enemy the devil prowls around like a roaring lion looking for someone to devour. (I Peter 5:8)

We have a very active enemy. Knowing this should help us to answer the question, How should we then live? We must have the correct mind-set that will lead us to conclude that it's not the world's way, but God's way.

Our society will tell you to get all you can, can all you get, and then sit on the can. (That's a little gem I heard from a good friend of mine Pastor Kenny Grant). That is where most of us are going. Society will also tell you that you need to keep up with the Joneses. (That couple has caused more trouble for us than any other!) That always seems to be the measure, doesn't it? It's all relative, and you and I always seem to want to do better than the guy next door or the person down the block. A gentleman by the name of George Fooshee once remarked: "People buy things they do not need, with money they do not have, to impress people they do not even like." I am willing to take a step further than that: The people that you are trying to impress do not even like you! So why all the effort and fuss to impress one another? Because of a worldly mind-set that needs to be <u>corrected</u>.

God has a different perspective for us that is found in I Timothy 6:17–19.

¹⁷ Command those who are rich in this present world not to be arrogant nor to put their hope in wealth, which is so uncertain, but to put their hope in God, who richly provides us with everything for our enjoyment. ¹⁸ Command them to do good, to be rich in good deeds, and to be generous and willing to share. ¹⁹ In this way they will lay up treasure for themselves as a firm foundation for

the coming age, so that they may take hold
of the life that is truly life.

In verse 17, we are told that those with means should
be *humble and not haughty*. Humility is being in touch with
what you cannot do. That is the perfect time to understand as
a believer, that whatever you can't do, God can do. Humility
leads to exaltation by God in due time (James 5:6). You need
to be humble about the money that you earn. The reminder
in Deuteronomy 8:18 is that God is the one who gives us the
ability to produce wealth. Therefore, you must recognize that *it
is not about you*. God gave you the power and the ability to earn
money, and if you get that twisted you will destroy yourself.

Paul also reminds those with means to be *hopeful and
not hasty* (v. 17b). You need to be hopeful in God, not riches.
If your hope is in wealth, you are actually being myopic, or
short-sighted. By hasty I mean that you are rushing to things
that offer temporary pleasure. Riches are here today and gone
tomorrow. Think about how many people are suffering severe
depression and fear their lives are over because of the investment losses they have sustained during the recession and stock
market plunge of 2008-2010? These things happen because
people not only have their money in the market, they have their
hope in the market. God says do not put your hope in wealth
because it will let you down. You cannot take it with you, and
your *next* trip will last infinitely longer than your current one!
Be hopeful and not hasty.

Paul continues in verse 18 by telling the rich to be *helpful
and not harmful*. He commands that those with riches need to
do good. He also says that if you are rich in money that you
should also focus on being rich in good deeds. You should not
be rich before God with wealth, and not be rich before God

with good deeds. When you embrace this truth then you will be generous and willing to share.

Finally, Paul affirms that the wealthy need to be *holy and not hedonistic* (v. 19). Laying up treasure for yourself in the next life is truly a long-term view. It confirms an understanding of sacrificial living with contentment. The follow-through on that perspective is a progressively sanctified life. Hedonism is about satisfying yourself to excess and complete indulgence. If you have means, you are in a better position to have many of the things your deceitful heart (Jeremiah 17:9) desires. Instead, send your treasure on ahead by investing in God's people and the ministry work of the kingdom.

You do not know anything about living until you start living according to kingdom principles. Correction to God's way from the world's way must be made first.

Add A Dash of Reflection

The second thing is we should live our lives with *reflection—not on today, but on eternity.* In Hebrews 11, we see Moses making some conscious choices that properly mirror the maxim: focus not on today, but on eternity.

> **24 By faith Moses, when he had grown up, refused to be known as the son of Pharaoh's daughter. 25 He chose to be mistreated along with the people of God rather than to enjoy the pleasures of sin for a short time. 26 He regarded disgrace for the sake of Christ as of greater value than the treasures of Egypt, because he was looking ahead to his reward. (vv. 24–26)**

Moses knew it was all set up for him, since he was growing up as the son of Pharaoh's daughter. However, he chose the long-term view— passing on the pleasures of sin today, he chose to pursue God's plan, which would echo throughout eternity. He was looking ahead to his reward.

You and I must start thinking long-term. Long-term is not ten or even twenty years. Long-term is *eternity*. Eternity is where you will spend the majority of your life. Life is not over when you die. There is a transition. Either you will transition to hell to live forever with your sins, in separation from God, or you will transition to heaven, to be with God in glory. (That choice has everything to do with whether or not you accept Jesus Christ as your personal Lord and Savior). The right question is, "How will what I do effect eternity?"

Sprinkle In Selection

Third, we should live our lives with *selection–not to excess, but for enjoyment*. God does indeed want you to enjoy what He blesses you with. He is not a God who muzzles the ox while it is treading out the grain (Deuteronomy 25:4), so He wants you to eat and enjoy while you work. But that leads us to the question of the appropriate standard of living. You can't do everything, but you can do something. You can't go everywhere, but you can go somewhere. You can't buy everything, but you can buy something. Remember that you should always live like a steward. Don't be wasteful just because you have greater resources. If you have your eye on an item and you hear that it is going to go on sale soon, wait. Just because you could pay full price does not mean you should. Or say you want to go to Jamaica for vacation. You could properly plan the trip in order to obtain the best air fare and see if there are any other savings of which you could take advantage. Alternatively, you could just head to the airport tomorrow with no luggage, pay an exorbitant last-minute fare and plan to buy whatever you need once you arrive on the island. Needless to say, the second trip would cost significantly more. Even if you have the resources to do something like that, that would not be the act of a steward.

You should not waste the money God has given you. If there is an advantage in waiting, wait. If you can save money, save it. That is how a steward thinks.

Of course, a really good starting place for your standard of living should be consumption at only 40 percent of your resources. That is a threshold you should cross first. At that point you are consuming only 40 percent of what you take in, honoring God with your resources, handling your responsibilities as citizens of heaven, moving away from greed, and marching toward contentment. That is a pretty good place to be.

Once you are executing all of the elements of the money recipe, it is perfectly acceptable for you to continue to wrestle with this question of lifestyle. It will vary with the individual. For example, there is no hard-and-fast rule that says once you make $200,000 a year, you should only do the following things with your 40 percent set aside for consumables. Seek God's wisdom about your spending. He may be leading you to increase your giving or to support a family member in a meaningful financial way. God does desire that you enjoy what you have, but always keep a mind-set of generosity. If you remember to consider others (Philippians 2:9) you will be just fine.

Put In A Pinch Of Direction

Fourth, live your life with *direction–not what I say, but what God says.* Do you want to know what God said about a particular subject or have a particular situation where you don't know what to do? My experience is if you ask Him, He will tell you. If you pray and seek His face for an answer, he will give you an answer. It may be hard for you to *hear* His answer, especially if you really want to hear yes when He is telling you no, but He will give one. Joshua, for instance, asked a simple question of the Lord (Joshua 5:14): "What message does my Lord have for his servant?" If you want to know how you should be living or what you should be doing, ask your Lord.

Stewardship is about accountability, and accountability includes on-going relationship and continuing communication. You can <u>never</u> get to a place in your life where things are on auto pilot. God is interested in absolutely everything that you and I do, and He desires that we keep in constant communication with Him in order to strengthen our relationship. He wants to give us the right direction for our lives.

Mix in Some Connection

Fifth, we should live our lives with *connection–not just for me, but for others*. You and I should constantly look for opportunities to be generous to others. Tithing is a beginning, not an end. Increasing our giving and sharing our resources with worthy ministries within the body of Christ should be two of our goals as we move forward in our Christian walk. We also should desire to share our experiences with others as a source of encouragement. As God brings you through a financial storm and helps you to become a good steward over His resources, you need to shout it from the mountaintops. Why? Because your brother or sister needs to hear it. Since you've had the test, you need to give the testimony. God never wastes a hurt or an experience so expect him to use what happened to you for His glory and our good (2 Corinthians 1:3-4).

We are connected. The connection we have should extend beyond our own generation to different generations, especially to the generation that is coming after us. We have an opportunity right now to train up a generation that will honor God with their money. Just like with compound interest, don't underestimate the power of an early start. If we began at a young age to ensure that our children properly manage their money, it will stay with them and become a part of their character when they grow up. They must understand and implement the money recipe even with their limited resources. When your children receive money (birthday, Christmas, babysitting, paper route) do they honor God with a tithe? They should. If they do it now, it increases the chances that they will do it when they manage greater resources. Do they save a portion of their money? They should.

In order to encourage savings with our children, we told them to give us a portion of their money (we suggested 20 percent) and we would put it in the bank for them. If they did not touch it, at the end of the year we would double it. If they made one withdrawal, the annual doubling would stop. It has been several years since we have done this and guess how many withdrawals our four children have made in that time? None. No matter what they <u>think</u> they want, it never seems to be worth losing the savings incentive we have put in place.

When I was growing up, my mother put some money away in two mutual funds, one for me and the other for my sister. Somehow we found out about it (I think we opened up a statement that came to the house), and every time we wanted something (clothes, gadgets) we were clawing and scratching at my mother to get that money. My mother always told us, "No, that's not what the money is for." Year after tear we begged for the money, and year after year, Mom said no. Well, when I got married, guess who *finally* gave me *my* money?

Mom was right on time. If she had not been patient for me, I would not have had what I needed when I really needed it. Not for clothes or tape recorders, albums or roller skates, but to invest in the future of my new family unit. That is what we must teach our children. Waiting is worth it. Savings matters. Honoring God is important. That is the connection that is so desperately needed. As we know better, we have to do better. We must have a disciple-making mind-set. Each one must reach one. If we all do our part, we can break this cycle of bad money management. One of the key elements of discipleship is *illustration*. There must be illustration before there's *imitation*. Your kids need to *see* what you want them to be. Only then can they imitate that behavior. Only then can there be *impartation* to someone else. That is the true beauty of the discipleship process (2 Timothy 2:2). Just like the Energizer bunny, discipleship keeps going and going and going. That is the connection we need. It is not just about you, it's about others.

God answered the people's question to Ezekiel "How should we then live?" by declaring,

> **`As surely as I live, declares the Sovereign LORD, I take no pleasure in the death of the wicked, but rather that they turn from their ways and live. Turn! Turn from your evil ways! Why will you die, O house of Israel?'** **(Ezekiel 33:11)**

You do not have to stay in the state that you're in. *You can turn*. That is what God is saying to you and me. He is saying simply turn and *live*. Determine to honor God with your resources and start now. You can be a good steward over your time, your talent, and your treasure if you choose to be. Turn and live!

Father, in the name of Jesus, we thank you for the clarity of your Word. We thank you Father, for truth and we thank you for wisdom. We thank you Father for sensitivity to your Spirit and we pray for the strength to follow your lead. It makes our task easier in that we know better how we should live. It also makes our task harder, only because if we know better, we must do better. Father, thank you that you have revealed principles for us to follow in your Word and that you have not left us without divine instruction. We have confidence that as we have questions about anything in particular as it relates to our financial situation, we can seek your face and ask you and you will give us an answer. James 1:5 tells us that if any lack wisdom, he should ask you and you will give generously to all without finding fault. We thank you, Father, for being a full-service God. You never leave us hanging. You never leave us without instruction. You never leave us without a demonstration of your care. You always provide where you guide, and you always protect where you direct. Help us to honor you as stewards. May what we do edify the body, magnify your works, and glorify your holy name. In Jesus' precious name we pray, Amen.

Discussion Questions:

1. After reading this book, what would you say are the main differences between the way the world handles money, and the way God wants us to handle money?

2. How can you develop a mind-set of eternity with your finances in this life? What does it look like to store up treasures in heaven instead of on earth?

3. Do you enjoy your money with extravagance or with stewardship? What are ways you can be responsible with your money even in enjoyment?

4. How can you invest in the future of your children and grandchildren financially? What are some steps you can take to teach your children how to handle money?

CPSIA information can be obtained
at www.ICGtesting.com
Printed in the USA
LVHW011942231220
674975LV00012B/1045

9 781632 219923